RENTAL PROPERTY INVESTING

THE ESSENTIALS FOR EXPERIENCED INVESTORS

- How to Build a Smart and Unshakeable Wealth -

Mathew Li Zahng

3

© Copyright 2019 by Mathew Li Zahng -

All rights reserved.

This book is provided with the sole purpose of providing relevant information on a specific topic for which every reasonable effort has been made to ensure that it is both accurate and reasonable. Nevertheless, by purchasing this book you consent to the fact that the author, as well as the publisher, are in no way experts on the topics contained herein, regardless of any claims as such that may be made within. As such, any suggestions or recommendations that are made within are done so purely for entertainment value. It is recommended that you always consult a professional prior to undertaking any of the advice or techniques discussed within.

This is a legally binding declaration that is considered both valid and fair by both the Committee of Publishers Association and the American Bar Association and should be considered as legally binding within the United States.

The reproduction, transmission, and duplication of any of the content found herein, including any specific or extended information will be done as an illegal act regardless of the end form the information ultimately takes. This includes copied versions of the work both physical, digital and audio unless express consent of the Publisher is provided beforehand. Any additional rights reserved.

Furthermore, the information that can be found within the pages described forthwith shall be considered both accurate and truthful when it comes to the recounting of facts. As such, any use, correct or incorrect, of the provided information will render the Publisher free of responsibility as to the actions taken outside of their direct purview. Regardless, there are zero scenarios where the original author or the Publisher can be deemed liable in any fashion for any damages or hardships that may result from any of the information discussed herein.

Additionally, the information in the following pages is intended only for informational purposes and should thus be thought of as universal. As befitting its nature, it is presented without assurance regarding its prolonged validity or interim quality. Trademarks that are mentioned are done without written consent and can in no way be considered an endorsement from the trademark holder.

TABLE OF CONTENTS

Chapter 3: Identifying Rental Properties – Locally and out of State

Chapter 4: Growing Your Business in Real Estate Investing

Chapter 5: How Today's Technology Can Keep You Informed

Chapter 6: Managing Your Rental Property Finances

Chapter 7: Your Responsibilities and Legal Rights

. Landlord Responsibilities

. Landlords and Rental Responsibilities

. Legal Responsibilities of the Landlord

. State Responsibilities

Chapter 8: Handling Your Bookkeeping and Taxes

. Mortgage, Insurance and Property Taxes

Chapter 9: Dealing with Unexpected Rental Expenses

. Fire and Vacancies

Chapter 10: How to Create a Passive Real Estate Business

. Passive Real Estate Business Defined

. Mistakes to Avoid

. Ways to Create Passive Income

. Other Ways to Make Passive Income

Conclusion

INTRODUCTION

Now that you've been growing your real estate rental property business and are working at accumulating more real estate to create a profitable financial portfolio, you may not have had the time to learn all about the points of the other business you are in and that is being a Landlord. When you read this book, Rental Property Investing – The Essentials for Experienced Investors - How to Build a Smart and Unshakeable Wealth you will be able to increase your knowledge as a real estate investor, but also as a landlord to the tenants residing in your rental properties.

This book will help you understand the importance of being proficient in managing your properties, interacting with your tenants, continue to grow your rental business and identifying real properties. As you already know, real estate can be complex and now the risk is two-fold - because not only are you acquiring real estate rental properties, you are engaging with the people who occupy your rentals and who you are responsible for their safety and health while they are residents.

This book will provide you with a summary of how to manage and maintain your rental properties, how to today's technology can keep you up-to-speed on the latest real estate market trends, how to handle your rental property finances and, very importantly, your responsibilities and legal rights as a landlord.

Overseeing your rental properties is a full-time job within itself. This book was written in the hope you may benefit from all the information and resources provided.

How to Get the Most Out of This Book

This book has been written to work for you in a number of ways:

- Read the book entirely to acquire all the information you need to grow your real estate business as well as learn how to function in your other business as a landlord

- Read the book along with your duties as a landlord maintaining your rental properties as an investor, continuing to acquire rental properties and establish a profitable portfolio

- Use this book to help in researching markets to invest in as well as learn how profitable futuristically an investment can be

- To help you be a successful landlord who is aware of all the legal processes that are entailed in maintaining your rent properties

- To inform you of what you need to do in the event of a catastrophic event should affect your property when it happens, and during the aftermath

The key to having a well-rounded real estate investment business as well as the business as a landlord is to maintain the rental properties you already own as well as learn how investing to view the futuristic profitability of other real estate investments.

This book has been written for you to continue to build a profitable real estate investment business as well as navigate the business of becoming a landlord. You want both these businesses to generate a profitable, positive residual income and have your business thrive now and onward into the future.

CHAPTER I

How to Proficiently Manage Your Rental Property

Congratulations! You've become a rental property owner and are in the process of building your real estate rental property business. You've come a long way from when you first began to invest in real estate rental properties to now owning two or more.

You are now a landlord, whether you've invested in a single-family home, condo, or townhouse, and are responsible for the management and maintenance of your rental property.

Managing, and maintaining a rental investment property can be time-consuming, at times inconvenient, frustrating, demanding and, quite frankly, a headache. This is the part of investing that isn't the positive side.

After all the research, the searching for a property, the decisions, and the work you've put in that finally made your rental property possible, now comes the reality of ownership and all its responsibilities. You may still need to learn more in order to manage and maintain your properties, or to learn about new technology that will help you to achieve all the goals you have set for yourself and your real estate business.

When you learn to manage your rental property proficiently and stay on top of property maintenance, you will find that many of the situations that arise when maintaining a property can be controlled and kept to a minor level.

It's important to take care of your real estate property.

Just like anything else that you have in life, your rental investment property needs special care to be profitable and successful and continue to remain that way.

PRE-RENTAL STEPS

You're ready to rent your property. Take note of the steps needed to be taken in order to attract qualified tenants and finally rent the property.

Rental properties need continued attention to ensure they will be the positive revenue asset that you wish for them to be. The process to have your property ready to be listed and rented are numerous.

- The property must be totally repaired and complies with all the codes of the state, county, and city the rental is located. Only after the property is compliant can it be listed as a property for rent

- Advertise the property in the local newspaper, social media websites or list it with your real estate agent if you don't have time to show the property or take any of the phone calls you will be receiving inquiring about the property.

- The agent will list the property on the Multiple Listing Service (MLS), take the calls and schedule the showings.

- If you decide to handle the showings yourself, schedule appointments to show the property to prospective occupants. Explain the length of the tenancy and the monthly rent, as well as the initial deposits (security and first month's rent that will be required. Some landlords require the last month's rent as well. This is entirely up to you to decide how many upfront costs you are going to ask for the rental).

- Ask if the renters have a pet and if so, what kind of pet it is. Let them know there is a pet deposit that is separate from the security deposit on the property. Confirm the date that the rent is to be paid and is considered late after that date. Let the renters know if there is a grace period after the rent is due. Usually, it is 3 to 5 days, with a late fee charged after the set date of the grace period.

- The rent payment is key in paying down the mortgage, so any grace period given should not overlap the day the mortgage payment is due.

- Communicate with the prospective occupant clearly so there is no misunderstanding in what they are being told. The rental agreement will have all this information included which, once they sign it, will bind them to the terms of the contract.

- Have the application for the rental filled out by the renters. Each applicant who will be named on the lease should fill out a separate application.
  A fee will be charged for each application to cover the payment for the background check.

- Review all applications. You want time to decide which applications are the ones you feel merit moving forward with and taking the next step in the process.

- Your next step is having a background check run to screen the applicants' information. There are companies that can perform this service for a nominal charge. This will be paid for by the fee charged to the applicants' application fee.

- If the applicants pass the background check, you are free to offer the property for rent to the prospective occupants.

- Have a contract drawn up for the rental. There are many forms of rental contracts online that you may want to use and review to add in any of your own stipulations for the renter to follow. If you are using a real estate agent, they have a rental contract agreement that can be used. Whichever form you want to use for a contract, review it and make sure you are satisfied that it covers everything you want to include in it for the tenants to abide by.

- Schedule a day to have the contract signed. Collect all the deposits in a bank check or post office or bank money order. Money orders from a retailer, such as a 711 have become more of a risk due to fraud. Give a receipt to the tenant of all deposits received. Confirm the tenants' move-in date and schedule a walkthrough.

- Take the opportunity for you or the real estate agent to review the date the rent is due. Make sure the tenants have set up their accounts for electricity, water, gas (if necessary) and if it is a single-family home, garbage pickup.

- Unless the utilities are included in the rent, all utilities must be in the tenant's name and any deposits they need to send for the opening of each of these accounts will be handled by each individual utility service.

- Take photos of the property and date stamp them to have a record of what the condition of the property is at the time of giving the new tenants possession. Do this a day or two before the walkthrough.

- Meet the tenants at the property to do a walk through before any furnishings are moved in. Take note of the condition of the property at the time of the move-in by the tenants.

Have a checklist for each room that includes the condition of walls, windows, doors and, in the kitchen, all appliances.

- At the end of the walk-through hand the keys to the tenants.

Maintaining Your Investment

<u>WHAT IS NEEDED TO MAINTAIN CONTINUED OCCUPANCY IN YOUR RENTAL PROPERTY?</u>

A real estate investment can be a benefit and can be the main source of your income. It can garner a cash flow that leaves them with a substantial amount of money even after all financial obligations have been paid.

People who own a real estate investment property have the opportunity of controlling the success of their property, or its failure. They can control their financial future.

Part of increasing your success and the benefits you gain from your rental investment property is learning how to maintain its upkeep. Keeping your property clean and neat is a plus that can be to your advantage. Your property will maintain its value when it's well maintained and attracts quality tenants, benefitting both sides. (Asad, Ranah, 2019)

INSPECT THE EXTERIOR AND INTERIOR OF THE PROPERTY

Maintaining your rental property to be damage-free and well-kept will increase the value of the property and have the ability to hold on to good tenants. Although there are unforeseen costs for repairs and replacements when these situations come about don't wait to fix them.

A list of the things you should look for when you're inspecting the property

The Interior

- Heating and air conditioning – Inspect the heating and cooling system on a regular basis. Check the filters, and make sure there is no foliage growing around them. The airflow can be restricted and may ruin the system, which adds up to a costly repair.

- Paint – Check to see if there is any paint chipping or mold that may be on the walls. Always repaint to provide a fresh and clean interior for a new tenant.

- Water heater- Make sure to remove dirt and drain the water heater. If the water where the property is located has an abundance of sediment, this may be a monthly check of the appliance.

- Smoke detectors – This is crucial. Check the smoke detectors and insert new batteries before new tenants move in.

- Check that they are functioning properly. Smoke detectors that aren't working properly can put your tenants in danger.

The Exterior

- Check the roof – If there are shingles that are missing, mold, moss or damaged flashing, the repairs should be immediate to prevent more costly damages in the future.

- Check to see if there are any tree limbs or other foliage that are resting on top of the roof. If so, have them cut back. They can do damage to the roof, and look unsightly to tenants.

- Exterior paint and siding – Have the exterior of the rental property painted so that it is protected from the sun damage and moisture that can damage the property. Any damage to the exterior, faded paint makes the property look faded, old, and uncared for. No one wants to live in this kind of house.

- Windows – Check that all the windows are properly sealed with no gaps. Seal any gaps you may find. This will prevent moisture damage and the loss of heat in the winter and air conditioning in the summer.

- Landscape – Look for trees with fungus or broken tree branches. Make sure the grass is healthy and mow it so the property can be seen as well-maintained.

Who Fixes What?

Having repairs done is costly and a necessity to maintain your rental property to its highest level. In order to keep the property in good condition, you will need a network of professional contractors and handymen to do the work needed when it's necessary.

To avoid confusion of who should be doing what repairs, it's the little jobs that sometimes need more attention than the major repairs.

- Have the numbers of at least two handymen at the ready to take care of any simple repairs that need to be performed. Any maintenance issues need to be addressed and remedied.
  For example, if the garbage disposal becomes clogged or the water heater reaches an age that it needs to be replaced and installed, have a handyman take care of these issues as quickly as possible. It is possible when you purchase a new appliance like a water heater, that the installation is done by the people who deliver it.

Whenever you are purchasing a new appliance, like a water heater, refrigerator, or a stove, check to see if they will be installed by the people who deliver them.

- Any work that needs to be addressed, such as plumbing issues, air conditioning or electrical problems should be dealt with by licensed contractors who are specialists for these kinds of repair.

Happy Tenants

Keep your tenants happy while they live in your rental property. It's not all about fixing the damages, but also checking in every now and again to see how everything is and asking if there's anything they need.

How many times have you heard the words "my landlord is the best?" Not often if you ask most tenants. If you show your tenant that you're interested in their well-being and that they and the property are a priority, word-of-mouth will have people seeking your properties out for the opportunity to rent and live in them.

One of the main reasons tenants move out (or take landlords to court) is they are unhappy with their living conditions.

Of all the places a tenant wants to be able to feel happy and safe is in their home. If it doesn't make them feel that way, they'll leave.

Hire a Property Manager

This chapter began with how caring for a rental property can be a daunting task. It is a job unto itself. If you feel that managing the property is too much for you to handle, or you're handling it badly, it's time to hire a property manager.

Property managers are specialists in maintaining real estate rental property. It is costly, but the time you save can free you up to working on expanding your business 90% of the time instead of only the 10% you can spare when you're managing your rental property on your own.

Property managers handle all the details of collecting the rent, making the necessary calls, and hiring the contractors or the handyman to make repairs, check the exterior and interior of the property and report it back to you for your approval.

There is more about property management companies over the course of this book.

Improve the Property

People who rent properties to live in look for new and upgraded rental properties. As the owner of a rental property, renovating and improving your property should be part of the care you take of the rental property.

Modernizing the interior by installing new lighting fixtures or upgrading all the doors or sprucing up the yard by creating a garden or planting flowering bushes are ways you can improve the property.

Research the kinds of changes you can make that are affordable. These are small changes that can enhance the look of your property and attract tenants. (Asad, Ranah, 2019)

Maintenance When a Property Is Vacant

The maintenance of your rental property will be a never-ending cycle of repairs, inspections, and unexpected situations that will arise. The one thing that can prevent many maintenance issues is by taking preventative measures and immediately remedy any problems.

- If your investment is a single-family home and your tenant has moved, you now have a vacant property to care for until you find your next tenant (actually, they'll find you).

  While you're waiting for the right renter to apply to rent the property, there are items that need to be taken care of until the new tenant has moved in.

- The lawn needs mowing and the exterior of the property should be maintained. Any mail the old tenant is still receiving at the property needs to clear out of the mailbox as quickly as possible. Contact the former tenant and let them know that their mail needs to be forwarded to their new address.

The main reason the property needs attention while it's vacant is that you don't want to let people know the house is vacant. Overgrown grass and mail piled up in the mailbox and on the ground in front of the front door are dead giveaways that no one is home. You want to prevent vandals from destroying the property, stealing appliances and other items they can get their hands on.

The other group you want to deter are squatters who won't mind making themselves at home. Squatters can be a major problem because they can go as far as having the locks changed so you can't get in.

Getting them evicted may be as simple as calling the police, but if they've dug in and you finally become aware of their tenancy way after they've moved themselves in, you may have to go through the legality of eviction through the court to get rid of them.

Visit the property at least once a week to check on it.

If you have neighbors who you trust and keep in touch with or are using a real estate agent to list the property, ask them to call you if they see anything suspicious. You may want to park a car in the driveway if there is one that you're not using or ask a neighbor to park a car there in order to deter anyone who may be curious about the house.

Responsibilities of a Landlord

Transitioning from being an investor to becoming a landlord who manages and maintains their investment property is a new experience and responsibility. A rental property needs to be maintained in order to derive the positive cash flow that you wish to gain from it.

The responsibility of becoming a landlord for a rental property encompasses the maintenance of the property as well as the health, happiness, and safety of the tenants occupying it.

Stay up-to-date on Tenant-Landlord laws to help in maintaining your rental property. You want to have it managed correctly.

Even if you have a property management company working for you and they are required to know tenant-landlord law, you should be as knowledgeable because this is your property and all the final decisions about the property and any legal penalties or fines all fall on you.

Tenant-landlord law gives a structure for you and your tenant to follow and avoid any misunderstandings or mistakes.

Under this law, a landlord is obligated to maintain the property to be in a condition that is habitable.
Learn about tenant-landlord rules and laws that are set by your state in order to be on the right side of the law with regards to evictions, as well as all tenant-landlord rights and responsibilities.

Your tenants have the right to enjoy a habitable living atmosphere.   The responsibility is for the homeowner to maintain and take care of the property. A well-maintained property will enable you to increase your cash flow and have a successful rental. (Asad, Ranah, 2019)

If rental property issues arise, as they will always do, work to resolve them before they become bigger, less controllable, and more problematic so everyone wins.
As a real estate investor, you have decided that you are investing in rental properties to create a profitable passive income that you want to grow into a business.

The next chapters will help you learn as much as you need to be able to grow your business as well as maintain your properties, so they remain profitable and manage your tenants and their needs.

CHAPTER 2

How to Interact with Your Tenants

You're the owner of rental properties and a landlord to the tenants who occupy them. As an investor, you're involved in the real estate industry, but as a landlord, you are in the business of dealing with people.

Finding, interacting with, and managing tenants is where the reality of your rental property comes alive. Developing a good relationship with your tenants is imperative to the success of your rental property business. You can have a great rental property, but without tenants, you really don't have an occupied rental.

You probably had a long thought before you entered the rental property business about the stories you heard of tenants who can, to put it kindly, annoy you. Tenants who let their pets (and themselves) run amuck and destroy the property, or demand middle of the night repairs or disappearing in the middle of the night owing you more than a month's rent and leaving all their garbage behind for you to have cleaned up.

So, besides having your tenants screened properly to weed out the tenants can be nightmares, you can avoid the problems by learning how to treat and manage your tenants.

How to Treat Your Tenants

How to treat your tenants is a very simple concept – treat them as you would want to be treated. Simple and basic, treating your tenants with this in mind will go a long way.

If you've ever rented someone else's property, how were you treated? The answer would probably be not very nicely, or as an address/apartment number with very little interaction with the landlord.

A landlord who arrives at a tenant's home at 8 am on a Saturday morning unannounced and says the handyman needs to replace some of the ceiling tiles that you had complained about six months before. The tiles have been falling down from the ceiling affected by any movement or slight vibration in the house.

The tenant complained that they tried contacting the landlord for months about the problem and either got sent to voicemail or when they did speak on the phone, the landlord was always interrupted by "another call coming in; they'll call the tenant back" and they never do.

The landlord let themselves into their tenant's residence when they weren't at home and allowed their kids to rummage through the tenant's kitchen cabinets and drawers and helped themselves to the food in their tenant's refrigerator.

There was a mess left in the kitchen to top off the intrusion that really didn't have any explanation as to why it happened.

These instances display no respect for the tenant's quality of living in the property, their privacy, and their property.

This is unacceptable behavior on the part of a landlord.

A 24-hour notice to tenants before you stop by to do any repair work or just to see how things are going is a courtesy that should be offered to the tenant.

Of course, in the case of an emergency like a flood, or a fire, this rule doesn't apply.

It is also imperative to contact the tenant within a 24-hour window to respond to a phone call, text or email that is sent by the tenant requesting attention to an issue.

Communicating with Your Tenant – Be Polite!

Be polite. You are dealing with people and all sorts of personalities. Be professional and courteous. Getting angry at your tenant may not be the best of ideas, particularly if they're locked into a long-term lease. Take the high road.

There is no problem that warrants being rude or screaming at your tenant. If you don't like or want them to scream at you, don't scream at them.

This is not to say that some tenants don't communicate with their landlord by screaming or being nasty. Unless you have not lived up to your responsibilities as a landlord and the tenant is beyond frustrated, the screaming, name-calling, and nastiness is an unacceptable way to communicate.

If that is their way of communicating, you need to set the boundaries and let the tenant know that any screaming,

name-calling, or nastiness in speaking with you is unacceptable and it doesn't get the problem resolved.

Let the tenant know you will be more than happy to speak with them and resolve any problem they want to be fixed by speaking in normal tones and with civility. This is how you prefer to communicate and appreciate that they do the same.

Don't ignore any repair requests that are made. Tenants grow frustrated and, eventually, angry because they are ignored by their landlord and the repair is not made. Meanwhile, they're paying rent while whatever needs to be repaired is an inconvenience to them. This doesn't make for warm and fuzzy feelings from the tenant.

Keep a Record of Everything

Keep a record of everything. Every communication, preferably email because it is written documentation of any request, should be kept in each tenant's electronic file. This should be the main form of communication. E-mails serve as a shield between you and the tenant and give you a bit of privacy. An email arriving late at night can be responded to in the morning.

Some people like to send texts but discourage that form of communication. It can't be entered into the electronic file folder for the tenant.

You probably can, but it takes time to do so and you don't need to take extra time to figure out how to transfer a text to an email.

Some tenants may insist on using texts and ignore the email mandate. Let these texting diehards that you do not read text messages and they will not be accepted as valid communication to you or your staff.

Limit phone calls for absolute emergencies only. Multiple phone calls late at night are annoying and intrude in your private time. Your tenant has after-hours from their job and the same should be afforded to you from your job.

Inform your tenant in writing when they sign the contract what the communication parameters are so there are no misunderstandings.

Another reason for emails is to validate every communication that you and your tenant send to one another. This way if a tenant ever complains or files an action against you, you have all the documentation you need to support your responses and attentiveness.

It can also protect you if a tenant states they sent you an email to end their tenancy by giving you a 30- or 60-day notice and there is no email documenting their notice.

Be Responsive to Your Tenant

Remember that you're dealing with people.

It's important to be responsive and communicative.

Tenants want to know that you're listening to them and that they've been heard.

For example, you receive an email that asks that a few of the windows need their seals replaced because the tenant is losing heat and can feel the drafts coming from the windows.

Keep your tenant updated. Although you or your staff are working to get someone out to the property to resolve this problem, keep the tenants updated on the progress being made. The tenants are not aware of what goes on in the process of contacting a contractor and making the appointment to get him out to them. Not hearing from you for over three days may give them the idea you forgot or that you just don't care.

Actively communicate the information about the contractor who will be coming to fix the windows. If the contractor can't make it for two days, let the tenant know this. Send your tenant an email and telephone them to remind them the day before the appointment when the service will be performed.

This may seem like over-communicating, but it will always pay off in the long run. If you have good tenants and they appreciate the way they're treated by you and your staff, they will continue to rent the property.

However, your courtesy should not be extended for every request the tenant makes. Don't allow your tenants to walk all over you. They may be paying the rent, but you are the owner.

Tenants are well aware of the stories of landlords who are not the best and would rather live in a rental where they are treated with courtesy, respect, and responsiveness.

Tenants who are Irritating

You will, sooner or later, have a tenant who irritates you to no end; a tenant that really is annoying. No matter what you do or how much you do, these "divas" are never satisfied, constantly complain and, even when the latest problem is resolved, have a whole new problem at the ready to complain about.

Even if this type of tenant gets on your nerves every time you receive a new email complaining, you need to continue to treat them with respect and professionally.

Take a step back and calm yourself when a tenant tests your patience. Never respond to a tenant if you are aggravated or angry. Don't allow them to irritate you and remember to treat them as you want to be treated.

More Problem Tenants

If all is going well with your tenant, then consider yourself fortunate. However, if there are any issues that arise during their tenancy, you need to take steps to nip problems in the bud early on or take action to protect your investment.

Investigate any complaints that are made by the neighbors to your property, the Homeowners Association (HOA) or authorities because of disruptive behavior. You may personally hear about them, or your property manager may be contacted.

Speak with the tenants and find out what their side of the issue is. It is only fair to hear the tenant out and see if it isn't the neighbor who is the problem and is complaining about a small situation or a misunderstanding that can easily be resolved.

Whatever the situation, and it seems to be one that can be resolved, do so for everyone's sake. However, if it is your tenant who is disruptive, a warning needs to be given so they are aware that you are concerned and serious about maintaining a level of peace and goodwill with neighbors in the community.

If the tenant breaches the contract by partial paying or not paying the rent at all, serious disruptive behavior and property destruction by the tenants or their pets, you will find it necessary to evict the tenant.

If their rent is paid in full for the month, you cannot force them to leave before the month is up.

Additionally, they are entitled to their security deposit, minus any deductions for any damage or expenditure to clean and rid the property of any garbage left behind.

A letter detailing any deductions needs to be forwarded to the tenant within 30 days after they leave the property. Unless the damage is so extensive that the tenants' have forfeited their security deposit, a check for the remaining balance of their security should be sent. If their pet did not damage, they are to receive the pet security deposit as well.

The Property and Your Tenants

Hopefully, you have good tenants who are respectful of the property, pay their rent on time and are good neighbors.
The important monthly task is collecting the rent. However, as with the risk of owning a rental property, comes the risk that the rent may not be paid either on time or not at all. This is one of the biggest problems a landlord can have when owning a rental property.

Collect monthly rent. This can be arranged by supplying pre-addressed envelopes with your address or a Post Office Box address for the tenants to mail their checks.

If the tenant bounces a personal check, you need to have a bank check sent for the payment of rent in the future.

This will eliminate having to wait for a new check to be issued and fees that will be charged to your bank account.

Partial-payment or non-payment of rent – this is a serious problem because it impacts your finances and the mortgage payment on the property if it was financed for its purchase.
Contact the tenants to ask what the problem is and if this is going to be a continuing problem.   If there is a plausible reason for a partial payment, allow the one time.   A non-payment is a cause for eviction.

Hiring a Property Manager

Being a hands-on landlord isn't for everyone and that's fine. However, if you find taking care of your rental property overwhelming and too stressful or takes too much time out of your day.
If you want to keep a distance from the landlord process, you can hire a property manager as an alternative solution.

The responsibility doesn't disappear for the investor.
You are the owner and his landlord, and ultimately you still have to make decisions about the property.

A qualified and licensed property manager will take care of all the busy work that goes with maintaining a rental property. Hiring a property manager, the worry of directly interacting with tenants, scheduling repairs, dealing with contractors, or having to execute an eviction is eliminated for the investor.

The charge a property manager, or management firm bill to their clients is 10% of the monthly rent for a single-family home, and 4% to 7% for properties with 10 units or more.

If you are an owner of multiple properties, a management firm would be a good way to have all your properties are handled under one management firm. However, if you have one or two properties, for example, two single-family homes, a single property manager who works independently would be sufficient to service the two properties.

Rents are set by the property manager to attract renters.
They also collect the executing of all leases. Property managers are obligated to have full knowledge of the state and municipal laws.

A property manager in South Florida gives a few insights into what is needed to successfully manage rental properties.
With over 20 years of experience, she has managed single-family homes, townhouses, and fourplexes.
The main responsibility of a property manager is keeping the investor's investment maintained and managed.
This may sound easy, but when asked about some of the most problematic issues in maintaining a property, she noted a few instances that came immediately to her mind.

TENANTS – There are tenants who call for every little thing that happens, even as minor as a light bulb blowing out in the bathroom or hallway. Or a tenant who complains that it's hot and the air conditioning is not functioning property only to find the air conditioning filter hasn't been changed and refuse to purchase a replacement.

The tenant feels these are expenditures that the landlord should pay for because it's their property, not the tenant.

HANDYMAN PROBLEMS – As was stated earlier in the chapter, having at least two or three telephone numbers for a handyman is really important. Most of the problems that arise at rental properties are small fixes – the garbage disposal gets clogged, a window blind needs replacing, or a door keeps sticking and is hard to open or close.

What happens is this – the property manager calls a handyman named Joe to do a job. Joe states he can be at the property on Thursday at 1 pm to get the job done. The day of the phone call between the manager and Joe is Tuesday.

The property manager's next phone call is to the tenant to let them know that the problem they want to be fixed will be done on Thursday at 1 pm. The property manager asks if the tenant will be home. They will not; they're working and won't be home until after 6 pm.
The property manager gets permission from the tenant to enter the property and wait while Joe fixes the problem and will lock up when it's done. However, this is when a handyman becomes a problem.

Joe doesn't appear at 1 pm. The property manager calls and texts asking where he is and how long will it be before he will be arriving. No answer from Joe. After an hour of waiting and no response from Joe, the property manager leaves the property. Now she has to call the tenant to let them know the problem wasn't fixed and get back to them when another handyman is able to do the job.

This is frustrating for the property manager and the tenant.
It's also a waste of time for the manager who has other properties to manage.
The property manager allows any handyman only one late arrival or no arrival. If it occurs again, their telephone number is deleted from her phone.

There are many other problems that this property manager pointed out – the wrong materials purchased by a contractor, contractors who don't do background checks on their employees which results in theft from the tenant's residence, and tenants who make it next to impossible to schedule a repair and insist on having it done on the weekend when most contractors charge more for their service.

Repairs and Costs

Decisions on how the property is managed and who works on any repairs or upgrades are made by the investor.

However, the property manager can recommend one of their contractors to do repairs.

Experienced property managers usually have contractors they have been working with for years who do excellent work and are reasonably priced. They will hire them to work on the property with the consent of the investor.

Property managers want to keep the investor as a client and make sure they are happy with the services they provide them.

Paying the Contractors

Contractors like to be paid on time.

Most contractors are independent business owners and their services are their livelihood.

An upfront deposit is what is usually required by a contractor before they begin a job. They are not in favor of running after the investor for payment for the remaining balance once a job is completed. If they are not paid in a timely fashion, the contractor, or the property manager who hired the contractor can get a lien put against the property in a court filing.

The lien is called a mechanics lien and will be recorded with land records and appear in a title search of the property. In other words, if the investor decided to refinance the property, the lien will appear as an unpaid lien that the investor needs to clear up before the property can be refinanced.

If the investor put the property up for sale and the title search shows a mechanics lien, the property cannot be sold until the lien is paid.

If you want to have contractors paid on time, have a company checkbook made available to the property manager to write checks for all services done by contractors and vendors that work on the property. Have the bank statement mailed to you at your residence or your office address for your review.

Paying the contractors on time is to your benefit.

They will remember you as an investor who pays on time and provides you with good service in return.

Property Budgets and Profit & Loss Reports

The budget for a rental property is managed by the property manager and must submit a Profit & Loss (P&L) statement to the investor. This report can be done quarterly, bi-annually, or annually depending on how the investor wants to see the information.

There are some investors who ask that their P&L be worked up and presented to them monthly.

The P&L is an outline of all the property finances – both income and expenditures. For example, if an investor wants to see the P&L for their properties, the P&L will show the income for three months (the monthly rent) and all deductions for expenditures such as any repairs, like a clogged garbage disposal, or supplies purchased, like the air conditioning filter, and all payments to a handyman or contractors.

This report will be the financial record that will be used when your taxes are due. If the investor does not have a separate accountant, the property manager will have one who will work up the tax report and file them for the investor.

A property manager documents all contracts and notes of all repairs made to the property and must have invoices to validate all expenditures. As an investor, you want to know where and how your budget is spent and what cash flow you have derived from your property.

The investor approves and makes the final decisions about all repairs and costs. A property manager can make decisions regarding any repairs only in emergencies without the investor's consent. This would happen if the tenants are in danger of being harmed, or the property is in danger of a problem becoming a larger and more costly one if action is not taken.

Evictions

Evictions are not the sunny side of rental property ownership. They are unpleasant for all parties involved. However, property management companies offer eviction services to investors for their properties in the event an eviction needs to be executed.

As stated earlier, non-payment of rent or other issues breaching the rental lease are grounds for eviction. The investor is conferred with before beginning legal proceedings.
The implementation is carried out by the manager or management company.

Some management companies file all documents with the court and have a management representative appear in court to attend the conviction proceedings.

Smaller management companies or independent property managers hire an eviction lawyer to file court documents and attend the proceedings. The lawyer charges a fee but frees up the manager who can't sit in court for one eviction when they are managing other properties. The fee charged is part of managing an investor's property and will be added to the P&L.

Eviction Process

- Serve a 3 day pay or quit notice to legally evict a tenant for no full payment of rent due after three days. That would include all rent that is in arrears plus rent that is due to bring their payments up to date;

- If the rental contract is breached for reasons that were included in the lease, the tenants can legally be evicted. A notice of 30 days should be given to the tenant;

- File the eviction notice at the courthouse;

- Contact a "server" and pay them to serve the tenants with the eviction notice;

- The court's process for eviction can take approximately 30-45 days and sometimes longer if there are any holidays on the court's calendar that will delay the process even further. While you're waiting for the eviction to be finalized, the property cannot be cleaned up and re-rented until it's vacant. This is a negative impact on your finances and cash flow;

- Have the property inspected after the tenants have vacated and have any damages repaired. Any damages to the property can be paid for by deducting it from the security deposit;

- Itemize all deductions from the security deposit and send a letter (not an email) via certified mail to the former tenants along with a check for the balance of the security deposit;

- If damages and the cleanup of the property is extensive, the entire security deposit can be used to make any repairs and bring the property to up to habitability to be rented once again.

  If the security deposit does not cover all the damages and repairs, the investor will be paying for the repairs out of their budgeted finances.

A letter to the former tenants still needs to be sent itemizing all the damages and the repairs needed to correct them and an explanation as to why their security deposit will not be returned to them.

Having a property manager establishes owning your rental property as a passive activity.

Managing your rental investment property is a formidable task. Whether you are a hands-on investor who enjoys doing repairs and manages your property personally as the landlord and has time to execute all the functions that are required of a landlord, or are an investor who is too busy to perform all the required functions of a landlord, a property manager is the smart way to have your property managed and maintained.

Focus on preserving the property, keeping your tenants happy, be proactive about the property's maintenance and its overall safe environment will allow you to gain the profitable returns for your efforts.

CHAPTER 3

Identifying Rental Properties - Locally and out of State

As a real estate investor building your rental property business, you want to invest in a property that will be a property that is in a good rental location, is in relatively good condition and will provide a positive cash flow.   Location and condition are two major factors in deciding if a property is worth purchasing.

Although price also matters, finding a property that will have minimal rehabilitation and repairs may not be easy.

As anyone who invests in real estate can say, purchasing an investment property with intentions of fixing it know that there are challenges and hidden issues that pop up and sometimes not recognizable even with the most thorough of home inspections.

Discerning a home at a first look to see if it is worth investing in takes experience and a sharp eye.

The major portion of this chapter applies to identifying rental properties locally as well as out of state.

The information you derive from each area you look to for rental properties is based on the part of the U.S. the property is located.

Some of the tips to determine if a property is worth the investment are:

Properties at a Glance

BUYING RENTAL PROPERTIES – When to buy rental properties is dictated by market cycles. These cycles will help you decide when to buy. To achieve this, recognizing if the location you're considering is a market that is apt to be more for home buyers or for home sellers.

If it is a home buyer's market, then it will be a good time for an investor to look for properties.
Of course, buying during a buyer's market is the best time to get a great rental property. A buyer's market is when the market has many homes available and not a great many buyers. This gives buyers all the control over the market.

RECOGNIZING GOOD LOCATIONS – Throughout the country, there are wonderful real estate markets. You can find sections of these markets on the threshold of growth in every state.
The identifying criteria you should look for:

- Located near a bit city – Large, populated cities offer a variance of jobs, accessibility of amenities, culture, and nightlife.

- **Population growth** – Invest in cities with a population of over 1 million residents. In areas this large and growing, renters account for 40% of the population, giving your rental property a cool 400,000 potential occupants for your rental property.

- **Buying a rental property in a large city Is Not A Must** - The main key to deciding the best neighborhoods is looking at the entire metropolitan area. Doing this may indicate that the suburbs, where schools are better, the crime rate is lower than the inner city and amenities provided are nicer and newer, has a greater need for rentals.
  Buying a property there would be profitable. However, don't buy too far into the suburbs as most people want to live no more than 30 minutes from the city.

- **Is the market a good one?** - Investors can make a decision if an area is undergoing a buyer's or seller's market by looking at the levels of inventory that's available and the length of time properties are taking to sell by the average days on the market (DOM). This data will give an indication of whether the market is a good one or not.

- **Demand for rentals** - Local property manager, real estate agents and websites like Zillow and Apartments for Rent can offer information about the demand for rentals in an area.

- **What is the average home price?** – Mid-range home prices are properties that are middle of the road. In a market that is affordable, the average price for a home should not be 3 to 4 times more than the average income of the residents of the community.

- **Home prices** – Are the prices for homes increasing or decreasing monthly?
  Research the trends of home values over a quarterly basis to get a feel for the home prices.

Locate the market and submarket – The most convenient investment may be a property in your neighborhood, but it may not necessarily be worth the money and time. The best market for your investment needs to be identified as well as the submarkets.

Submarkets are usually broken down into neighborhoods where a rental property will be the most profitable.
If the property is going to be managed personally by you, purchasing a rental property locally makes sense.
From the submarket information, narrow it down to the area's renters will usually look for rentals.

Any properties that have relatively easy access to major thoroughfares, highways and near public transportation are high on the list that renters to look for.
Using all the tools to find and purchase properties, a general area search on sites like Apartments.com or Zillow will show where the most common areas where rental properties are rented and the various ranges in rental prices.

Unless you are looking for a rare renter who is looking for an ultra-luxury niche neighborhood that is a distance from the more accessible downtown area, you will want to put more focus on a sub-market where there is more activity with new renters consistently moving in.

Student housing off-campus is an identifiable kind of rental property investment that enthuse investors.

Attention to properties that are close to the campus and are within walking distance are what investors tend to keep because of the demand for rentals make for higher rents.

While you're pinpointing submarkets that will produce the most demand with renters, also take into account the quality of the property you want to own based on what renters gravitate to and what is affordable for you.

Property classes are characteristically divided into three categories: A, B and C properties.

CLASS A – these are properties are top quality in the market, usually new and higher-priced

CLASS B – these properties are typically a little older but are maintained extremely well

CLASS C – these properties are older than the Class B properties and frequently needing to be repaired and renovated. Additionally, they're usually located out of the prime locations of real estate.

The age, design style, and renovation details can vary based on the location of the property. A New York City Class A property can't be compared to a Class A property in Des Moines, Iowa merely because the residents they attract are two different types.

Focusing on Class B or C properties may prove to be a better investment because while they may be work that would be required on the property, you can avoid reducing the potential pool of renters with a pricey rental rate.

Zoning, Liens, and Encumbrances
CHECK FOR ANY LIENS AND ZONING ISSUES –

These are two issues that can make a great looking property a "no" for investors. Zoning issues can create a problem.
Many local governments and their residents would rather have the actual property owners living in their community rather than tenants.
Actually, this is not a new concern for investors.
Municipal officials and renters have had many disagreements, whether for the short-term or over a more extended period. Many cases have been resolved by the courts.

Zoning laws can be a major obstacle for landlords. The laws can differ from one city to the other and may or may not be enforced.

Zoning laws are in place to set boundaries and limit particular kinds of properties to certain areas of a city. For example, a factory should not be within a residential community, and a commercial area, like a shopping mall does not have residential homes with their mall boundaries.

Zoning laws help populations exist with each other peacefully and limit conflicts and irritating calls.

Investors and landlords need to be especially careful not to run afoul of municipal zoning laws. These laws can change and any investor looking for rental properties need to be aware that a rental property can be completely legal one day but may not remain that way to infinity.

Owners who own large apartment complexes are more susceptible to the changes in zoning laws. Owning a multi-unit complex where a tenant or tenants have frequent visitors may have neighbors filing complaints with the local zoning municipality. The behavior of the tenants can invite zoning complaints, particularly if your tenants are running a business from your rental property. (All Business, 2019)

Some steps that can be taken to help you remain on the right side of applicable zoning laws:

- <u>Limit the activities of your tenants</u> – You can request that your tenants ask for approval before they begin running a business if the rental property is in a residential neighborhood.

A home-based business that doesn't result in continuous traffic and visitors shouldn't be a problem. However, if your tenant is running a nail salon from the property, the traffic from customers coming and going may generate a disturbance.

- **Familiarize yourself with zoning laws before you buy** – Become familiar with the zoning laws that are in effect locally before you purchase a rental property and continually follow up on any changes to local zoning laws. These changes may have an effect on your rental property.

  If other landlords are having problems with zoning laws in the area, it's possible to form a group to change laws that may be inhibiting your ability to profit from your rental property.

  Rather than a single person trying to effect a change in zoning laws, an effort from several landlords in the area will be more impactful with a zoning commission.

- **Be knowledgeable of your city's district** - You may not have a problem with zoning laws if the city where your rental property is located is divided up neatly into specified districts for residential, industrial, and commercial zones. (All Business, 2019)

  However, commercial sprawl continues to expand and the boundary lines are becoming a bit blurred and less clear. Apartment complexes are becoming located within industrial or commercial districts.

This may make it easier for tenants who work in the area to be attracted to renting one of your rental properties, but there may be zoning problems. This is important to think about before buying a rental property.

Investigate your rental property situation if you're not sure of how zoning laws may affect your rental and before you become involved in a zoning or legal battle.

- The potential of your property may be affected – A rental property that is located amid a noisy industrial or commercial district may have an effect on your ability to appeal to new tenants. Most people want to come home to peace and quiet, not to the sounds of industrial noise. It can be a real problem if there are industries that operate 24 hours.

The zoning it is in may affect the value of your property. If properties that are neighboring yours are in bad shape and unkempt because of the negligence of their owner, this can affect the property value negatively. This can be problematic if you plan to resell the property. What may have been a good investment, in the beginning, may decrease in value because of zoning laws. (All Business, 2019)

Liens Affecting the Property

Sometimes a good deal on a real estate property is too good to be true. When this happens, don't act too fast about making an offer on a property, you may find that there are encumbrances or liens applied against the property. It can be anything from a mechanics lien for non-payment of services to thousands of dollars in property taxes and fines for non-compliance to municipal codes.

You need to understand how encumbrances and liens play a part in your transaction.

An encumbrance is a claim against a property by anyone who is not the owner and can affect the ability to transfer the property. The free use of the property can be restricted until the encumbrance is resolved and lifted. (Chen, 2019)
Mortgages, property tax liens, and easements are the most usual kinds of encumbrances.

- An encumbrance may appear when there are other parties who still have an interest in the property.

- A restrictive covenant where a seller writes into a buyer's deed of the property that restricts how the buyer may use the property, such as the property may not be used as a rental. That kills any deal an investor would have in buying the property.

- However, it may be a restriction that is structural, such as the façade of the building must be left as is. As long as restrictive covenants do not break any laws, they can be as arbitrary or explicit as the parties want to agree to.

- Other reasons for encumbrances are property lines that are disputed, easements.

  If you are able to obtain the title by doing a quitclaim deed, the only interest in the property you get is the interest the seller has when the transaction is executed. (Landlord Station, 2014)

When there is money owed related to the property, a lien is recorded against the property.

- A previous owner may have had a judgment filed against them, or a fine by a homeowners' association or the city may have a lien on the property.

The discovery of encumbrances and liens are commonly found at a foreclosure sale or when a landlord gets ownership of a property by signing a quitclaim deed.
Title insurance policies can be a protective measure from these problems.
For example, an investor purchases a foreclosed property.
The lender may not have foreclosed on all the interest holder in the property and there is money that may still be owed to these people or companies. For example, if the prior owner had work done on the property and hired contractors to do the work,

the contractors could have filed a mechanics lien to make sure their work was paid for.

Another example is a condominium being purchased by an investor to turn into a rental property.

The property was a short-sale where the primary lender of the first mortgage agreed to take less than what was owed to them in lieu of foreclosing on the property entirely.

The investor hired a title company to do a search of the property and the deed. The title company discovered there were four liens on the property.

The IRS, the sister of the person who was selling the property, the first mortgage (who had already agreed to be paid less than what was owed to them) and a second mortgage who had not yet agreed to be paid less than was owed to them.

The property was listed with a real estate agent who negotiated with all four parties to accept a reduced payment of their claims. The sister refused as this was money, she could ill-afford to take less than the original amount, while the IRS and the lenders of the second mortgage agreed to a reduced financial settlement.

All liens were paid and resolved and the investor was free to purchase the property. For some investors, this may have been a property too problematic to purchase.

However, the property was being sold for $12,000 below the market value in a prime rental location and was in good condition with few repairs necessary.

The investor decided to see the sale through on the proviso that all liens were paid prior to the sale. If they had not been resolved, the investor could pull out of the sale.

Check to see if there are satisfactions or releases of any liens or encumbrances. These releases will be referenced by date and commonly by book or page number.

The number of the release must match the original number assigned to the liens or encumbrances that were found.

Records of the court can also be checked to check if any lawsuits were filed against the prior owner.

Divorces, foreclosures, and construction lawsuits are only a few of the kinds of lawsuits that become liens or encumbrances on the property.

If a property is in probate or guardianship this affect the title of the property. You may also look at the deed that the owner gained the title.

In order to protect yourself from potential issues that can arise can be indicated in the contract you submit to purchase the property. Be very clear in the contract that the seller must fix any problems before closing on the property. The responsibility is on the seller to give you the proof that the lien or encumbrance has been eliminated and removed.

If there are documents that are found indicating there may be an issue with the property, calling the party who filed the lien may simply reconcile the problem. There are times that the recording of the release is done in the wrong place, or even not at all. There are other times you may discover a serious issue that can only be solved by the seller or the legal system. (Landlord Station, 2014)

Other Identifying Factors

<u>The 1% Rule</u> - Some properties that investors purchase as rental properties can be evaluated by the 1% rule investment approach. This rule states that the property's purchase price should derive 1% of that price to be charged as rent, which will be the income the investor will yield as their cash flow.
(Bird, 2019)

<u>Example</u> – A 4 bedroom and 3 bath single family house is valued at $250,000 1% = $2,500. The property is in good condition in a highly regarded neighborhood that attracts quality renters.
The rental pricing is in line with rental rates for the same kind of properties in the neighborhood. This is a property that is a good investment.
Analyzing what the fair market rental costs are should be is part of an investor's due diligence in researching if a property they wish to invest in meets this rule.

The 1% rule isn't a hard-and-fast benchmark for all investors, it is a useful tool to screen and estimate how the cash flow will be derived from the property. It also sets a target rental rate if the property is presently unoccupied.
(The Roofstock Team, 2019)

There is also a 2% rule that can be applied in the same manner.

However, in many areas in the U.S., the 2% rule can usually be applied to properties that are not in great condition and are located in less than desirable areas.

A House with Good Potential - If, as an investor, you are interested in a property that is the worst property in the neighborhood, but is in a desirable rental area, is in need of upgrading rather than repair this is a property you should consider as a profitable rental property.

A property that can be upgraded over time yet may have an "old" interior look should not be a deterrent to having it used as a rental. This is a property that can be a profitable one that you'll miss out on if you pass on the purchase just because of outdated appliances and Formica countertops.

(Forbes Real Estate Council, 2017)

The Cap Rate - The price of the property/earnings ratio is the cap rate. This rate versus the neighborhood is a signal that the property may be a good property to invest in.

However, some sellers may legitimately more motivated than others to sell and possibly at a lower price point.

Another measurement is the price per door or price per square foot against the comps for the neighborhood is another method to measure when the data is used properly.

One other signal is that will define a property is a good rental investment are property price drops, a good indication that properties can be profitable.

Take Note of the Roofline - Take note of the roofline

it's the first thing an investor should look at. The roof is the storyteller of the house and will tell you if the house appears complicated, simple, durable, susceptible, well-designed, or weak.

Is the roof the original roof, or was it replaced? Is it added to or are portions of it patched? Will it properly drain?

If there's a chimney, is the flashing holding or are there portions missing or loose?

Make this the first part of the house you look at. Walk across the street and look at the roof from a distance. The roof tells a story about the property. (Forbes Real Estate Council, 2017)

<u>**The Condition of the Property**</u> - A determination can be made if a property can be purchased at a reduction based on the condition of the property and its presentation. If there are no online photos of the property it's almost safe to say the property is not attractive and has no curb appeal. Properties that have a few exterior shots but lack photos of the interior may fare somewhat better.

It also means the seller would be open to selling at a considerable reduction of the purchase price and the agent listing the property could be looking for a quick sale because there isn't much to work with.

Whatever the sense of the property's condition, visit the physical property to ascertain what the true condition of the property is, and whether, after rehabilitating the property, using it as a rental would be profitable.

County Appraisal vs. the Purchase Price - The address and the county appraisal district can determine if a property is a viable investment.   Go to the district website and enter the address.   If the purchase price is considerably lower than the county's assessed value, there is a 90% probability the property will be profitable.

The reason for this is the county determines fair market value by appraising the value of the property and adding 10-20% over their assessment.

Is the Price Less than 100 Times the Monthly Rent? -
If you rent out a property for $2,500 per month and it is within the rent price barometer for the area, the property you purchased for $250,000 is a good property is a good investment.

This barometer may simplify all the elements that go into investing in real estate, the price as a factor of 100 times the monthly rent is a fast way to obtaining real estate at a great price. (Forbes Real Estate Council, 2017)

Purchasing Out of State Properties

There is much to be profited from purchasing out of state properties and is a strategy many real estate investors use to add to their financial portfolio and gain positive cash flow.

Out of state rental real estate purchases is one of the major methods of accumulating wealth in real estate.

However, as with any real estate investment strategies, there are both pros and cons to be considered.

<u>Pros of purchasing out of state rental properties</u> - Buying a rental property in an adjoining state where the home prices are more cost-efficient than buying a local property where the home prices are more expensive is the most obvious reason to invest in out of state properties.

The price of investment property is a reasonable concern when you're investing in a real estate market. Prices relate with location, another reason why investors can definitely garner savings when investing in another area.

Investors are always looking for an income property that will be profitable.

Buying real estate that is inexpensive income properties, garnering a profit is the decisive goal of investing in real estate.

The return of investment is sometimes more profitable when you buy out of state properties, as well as rental income, cap rate and cash on cash return then properties within your own state. Location can affect many facets of investing in real estate including rental property profits.

<u>Cons of purchasing out of state rental properties</u> –

The distance of the rental property can be problematic. Overseeing and maintaining the property when you are an absentee landlord can create a myriad of problems.

If the investment is too good to let pass, and the property is too far for you to travel to on a consistent basis, hiring a property management firm will be the best way to have the property maintained and give the tenants the attention that's needed in the event any issues arise.

State laws in different venues regarding the housing market. You need to know what the housing and rental laws are in a state other than your own so you don't run afoul and end up paying fines that will impact on your profitability.

One needs to be extremely careful of out of state real estate investment scams that can rob you of your money and impact on your finances. If you want to invest in out of state rental investment properties, do business with a reputable real estate agent who is part of a national brokerage firm such as Keller Williams, Century 21 or Coldwell Banker Realty.

Always follow up with the real estate agent, have photos and a video walkthrough of a potential property shown to you in order to avoid any out of state investment disaster.

There is a great deal to grasp in identifying properties that can fill the bill of a real estate rental property.

Some investors skip some of the important steps when looking for properties that can make the difference between profitability or loss. Understanding zoning laws, job and population growth are critical when investing in a rental property.

There is a risk in real estate investing, but there are ways to mitigate and minimize the risks if you carefully review each new potential property investment.

CHAPTER 4

Growing Your Business in Real Estate Investing

It is profitable and rewarding to invest in real estate.

If you've just begun your real estate investment business, or have been investing for a while, growing your investment business is a process of deciding how you want to grow your business and what you wish to derive from it.

The reality of real estate investing is that you know it's important that your business makes money. You need to have enough capital to keep your business alive first before you can begin to think about purchasing an apartment building or that luxury vacation home in Santa Fe, New Mexico.

In order to grow your investment business in real estate, you need effective strategies on how to the make money you need to buy more real estate and garner positive cash flow from each property in your portfolio.

Right now, your focus has been on buying single-family homes, condos, and townhouses and you feel you're ready to move ahead and expand your horizons.

Here are a few tips to continue to grow your business.

Some of them aren't about purchasing properties, but ways you can locate properties off the beaten path, as well as furthering your investment education and credentials.

Expanding Your Real Estate Business

<u>Be more focused on networking</u> – A targeted approach to grow your business is attending networking events finding people to network with. When you attend an event, the goal is to interact with people who can be the most helpful to you.

This includes connecting with people to share advice with, or who can give you financial help.

When you learn this targeted approach, networking will be the most profitable for you. Concentrate on meeting with and developing a varied group of individuals and encircle yourself with people who can help in your reaching explicit business goals.

Commit to your purpose and business and, as these associations grow, think about how they fit into your business dealings. Someone may be more constructive in helping you expand your business while another person may best serve as a mentor. (Thiefels, Jessica, 2019)

<u>Form a Real Estate partnership</u> – Real estate investing is a costly business and buying multiple rental properties can be cost-prohibitive if you go it alone. You need to have the capital for the initial down payment on the property, plus all other costs incurred by the property during the purchasing process.

Everyone doesn't have large amounts of money on hand to invest in more than one property. However, there is a way to use leverage to increase your rental portfolio.

If you don't want to pay a mortgage by borrowing from a bank or private lender, you need how to search for a business partner who has the capital to invest.

When you find a reliable partner to help finance and grow your business quicker than waiting to save up the funds which could take months or years to achieve.

Combining your financial funds with a partner to purchase rental properties is a good solution.

Along with helping get the capital for your rental property investments, a real estate partnership can help with the responsibilities of managing and maintaining the properties. (Karani, 2019)

Obtain more Real Estate education – Probably one of the most important factors to expand your real estate investment business is to have the proper real estate education.

A real estate degree is not required for you to grow your rental property business, but you do need to obtain applicable knowledge and experience to improve the likelihood of your business success.

Since you've purchased and now own some rental properties you may have learned a few things but owning and managing more than one or two properties is quite a different scenario. You can't grow any further than one or two rental properties without upping your real estate education.

Graduating to multi-family dwellings or commercial rental properties can't happen if you bring your real estate education to a halt. To be successful in real estate investing, it's hard to continue if your education doesn't expand.

There are many ways to expand your real estate education. Online classes, YouTube videos, reading relevant real estate books, real estate magazines, news, blogs – the list goes on.

Learn about all you need to know. Here are a few examples of what is necessary to understand and be informed.

Become an expert in real estate market property analysis – Another important way to grow your rental property business is becoming an expert on how to handle both the real estate market property analysis when purchasing a rental property.

Your business may have a property or two that is generating positive cash flow at the moment, but in order to grow your business, you need to find several more to grow the business.

The factors of median income and jobs in the area will have an effect on the functioning of your rental property business. One of the ways your profits can be impacted by is high vacancy rates.

Because of this, you need to ensure that you do your due diligence and identify your rental properties and the markets you target are properly analyzed. Experiencing more than a few properties with negative cash flow is no way to keep a real estate business running.

Some investors may want to purchase properties near their homes. However, don't get stuck in a corner and think the only profitable rental properties are locally situated. Buying a property in another state can possibly be lucrative.

To help you identify real estate markets with greater rental property opportunities, real estate market analysis is a beneficial tool to integrate into the decision process.

When you have found a market that appears suitable for rental property investing, segment the area down to specific neighborhoods. (Karani, 2019)

How to develop a market analysis – This is also known as a CMA (Comparative Market Analysis) and is a study of properties and their value in the market that are current and are comparable to your property. This determines the value of the property in the market.

However, the appraised value differs from the market value.

An appraised value is determined by an appraiser's report.

The appraised value is determined by the condition of the property and is usually the value reported back to the lender.

Remember that the market value of the property is the one you decide upon after performing a CMA is subjective.

Developing a CMA may sound somewhat overwhelming because there are many factors you need to incorporate into the process. However, using an approach that is systematic and doing your due diligence to perform some steps, you will be able to conduct a CMA that will be of benefit to you.

<u>Property analysis</u> – This is how to analyze the property that includes both objective and subjective characteristics:

- Neighborhood and surrounding area
- Square footage and size of the property
- Land area
- How many bedrooms and bathrooms
- Other rooms (Living room, family room, kitchen)
- How many floors
- Age of the property (the year it was constructed)
- Amenities – such as a fireplace, balcony, patio, garden, swimming pool, etc.
- The convenience of location – schools, public transportation, major thoroughfares, shopping areas, etc.
- Any improvements to the area – road work, community center, cultural center, etc.

Identify some of the recently sold properties in the area within a 1-3 mile radius from your property that is comparable to the property.

Begin with homes sold in the past 3 months and, if there are not enough properties to compare to, look for homes sold in the past 6 months. For the CMA, find 3-5 homes that are comparable – location, the sizes of the properties, their age and other characteristics that are comparable to your property.
After you've drilled down to the number of comparable homes, look for homes that are actively listed for sale within the same 1-3 mile radius and single out at least 3 homes that are similar to yours.

When you find the homes that are comparable to yours that are listed for sale, realize this very important fact – the listed prices are not necessarily the real value of the property. Many sellers have higher expectations that the reality of the market and the condition of their property.

The market value of properties that are unsold becomes impacted by market trends. Properties being sold in the market their properties with, at times, over-inflated values.

If the sellers redid the kitchen, or installed a brand-new air-conditioning system, or put on a new roof, they tend to believe that the price of the property should reflect those improvements.
However, the market trend is what dictates the actual value of the property. Sellers want to increase the value of their property while the buyers try to negotiate a lower price. (Karani, 2019)
Use the listings that are active to complement the values of the properties that have been recently sold.

<u>Look at pending listings</u> – These are listings that are under contract but have not yet closed. Pending listings will be the barometer on how the properties in the market are performing at exactly the time you are doing your research.
Pending listings can be compared to the properties that are listed for sale and not under contract, as well as the properties that were sold 3 months ago. Have the prices for the pending listings increased over the sold properties?

Are they in line with the properties still for sale? Check the pricing and make sure the homes are comparable in size, number of rooms, etc.

Expired listings – These listings will be vital in helping your CMA. These are properties where the listing expired, probably because the price was considered too high for the property in comparison to other properties that were available.

There are a number of tools that can be used to conduct a CMA. A few reliable sources can be beneficial:

The website for the FHFA (Federal Housing Finance Agency) – This website has recent completed sales data contained in a region.

https://www.fhfa.gov/

The FNC Residential Price Index – There are more than twenty areas are major cities available. Home appraisals are the basis of the data in this report. This information is useful and gives information on the trends in any of the cities included that are covered and understanding what these trends are.

https://www.fncinc.com/products/rpi.aspx

Websites – Zillow.com, Realtor.com, and Trulia.com are websites that are good for checking what the real-time pricing is for active and sold listings.

Set your ceiling value by choosing one of the properties of the 3-5 comps you have found which is valued more than the property you are investing in.

This property may be close to public transportation, in a better location (not on a busy traffic street) or is newer in construction.

Choose your floor price which is a property valued less than your property.

Price range – the average of your ceiling price and your floor price will give you an average price range. Within this range is where your property should fall.

Compare your property to both the properties chosen and consider the age, amenities, size, renovations, upgrades, and location.   Look at the exterior of the sold homes and their neighborhood locations.

At the end of all these comparisons, determine where the property fits in the comparisons that you choose.

This will determine the value of the property in the market.

Now you have all the information you need about the property to decide whether it is worth investing in a rental property.

The next step into zero in on the rental properties for more valuation. To derive a positive cash flow and reduce expenses, real estate investors need to conduct an Investment Property Analysis. (Karani, 2019)

THE INVESTMENT PROPERTY ANALYSIS AND HOW TO DO ONE WILL BE COVERED IN CHAPTER 6.

Take a real estate exam – You can take a real estate exam to become a qualified real estate agent that is required by your state. It usually takes about two months to achieve.

The license gives you the ability to sell properties in the service to a larger company, or as an independent real estate agent. Most states oblige new agents to work under a broker for two-four years before they can become a broker. This is per the laws of the state you live in, so you need to check what this license allows.

What the license as a real estate agent will not allow is the ability to open your own firm and hire other real estate agents. You must become a broker and take the broker's exam in order to achieve this.

In some states, real estate "agents" are known as real estate brokers and a real estate firm is owned by a broker-in-charge. Again, check your state laws pertaining to real estate licenses.

Real estate brokerage firms take between 20%-50% of an agent's commission, so it's advantageous to become a broker yourself. You can earn all the commissions and, if you choose to hire other real estate agents to work in your firm, you get a percentage of the commissions from those sales as well. (Landau, 2019)

Locate off-market properties - You'll have a hard time making money if you can't find the deals before everyone else. Finding real estate deals that are going to be profitable has become a problem because there are so many investors looking for the same thing.

Many of the properties that you're going to find profitable won't be found on the usual sites like Zillow or the Multiple Listing Service (MLS). They'll be properties that owners need to sell as quickly as they can.

Some of them will not necessarily be foreclosure properties.

A "pocket listing" are off-market properties that may be owned by an owner who no longer wants the property, a home that was inherited and the owner has no use for the property or is leaving the country or a couple who are divorcing or going through hardship with their finances. These owners need to sell quickly and don't sell through the usual channels. There may be a For Sale By Owner (FSBO) sign on the property. (Landau, 2019)

These are the properties you'll want to pursue.

When you find an owner who is in need of instant cash gives you the opportunity to acquire a property below its market value. These are the properties that are going to be the most profitable and give you a bigger return on your investment.

One of the ways to find pocket listings is to keep an eye and ear out for them. There may be relatives, friends or acquaintances who will come to you to help them, either for themselves or for someone they know who is in need of selling their property quickly.

Another way to find these properties is by getting your name and business out to the people and groups that you can spread the word about your real estate investment business.

Join networking groups like Business Network International and the Chamber of Commerce. Someone from these groups or someone who they know may need to sell quickly, and they'll immediately think of you for the immediate help they need.

Other networks that you can develop are establishing connections with estate attorneys. They frequently have creditors who need to get to money quickly. Because of the situation, they'll be likely to sell a property at a discount.

Networking with wholesales is another way of purchasing discounted properties that are in need of repair, and almost as they are available, make a fast profit by selling them in a matter of days after buying them.
Wholesalers are in it for the short game. If you're a player who goes for the long game, this is a strategy that could be good for you.
Another way of purchasing a property is at auction. If you are comfortable with that idea, visit Auction.com. This site can be used to search for both commercial and residential real estate. Many of the properties on the site are priced below market value and listed on the site because they are in foreclosure or are bank-owned. (Landau, 2019)

Hire and partner with a knowledgeable real estate agent
You may want to work alone in your investment ventures.

However, working with a real estate agent can save you time and research and help you make good decisions in your investments.

There are real estate agents who specialize specifically in purchasing investment properties and have been working in the same locations for years.

They are valuable because they can locate those "pocket listings" and interact with other agents in the field who are knowledgeable about the property's investors are seeking.

A real estate agent can be your guide and help you grow your rental property business as well as analyze all the deals you may be interested in and help you close more deals.

You may need to work with more than one real estate agent based on the areas you target to invest in. You want agents who specialize in the markets that you are interested in investing in.

<u>Vacation rental market</u> – During the peak tourist season, owning a property you can rent to visiting tourists is an easy way to build equity in a great location. That's great for the season, but what do you do when the tourist season ends?

If you priced your vacation rental too high, the off-season for your rental won't be sought out by off-season tourists.

Over time, if the rental is left vacant during those off-season periods, they'll begin to add up, especially if you have a property manager overseeing the property.

The real cost off a vacation rental is managing and maintaining them. Remember, each time a vacationer leaves, the property has to be cleared and cleaned, all linens and towels laundered, trash is taken out, and bringing the rental to the level that it can be rented again.

If you want to have a successful vacation rental, the key is to have the property priced low enough that you have it rented year-round. If that not a possibility, make sure you can have it be profitable during the active season - this is vital.

Regardless of possible cash flow difficulties, a vacation rental property can be a great investment. However, before you rush and buy a vacation rental property, remember all the costs of maintenance, management, and repairs, all ongoing costs.

Are you capable of doing this in order to maximize the rate of investment?

Recognize and research all the variables when considering vacation rentals. If you can maximize profits during the season and manage and maintain the property and continue to derive a positive cash flow, this will be a great strategy to build your investment business. (Landau, 2019)

<u>Create leads with direct mailers</u> – Although you may think this is old school using snail mail, this method still works, particularly if you zero in on the market that you target is a desirable one. Research has shown that these direct mailers have the same ROI as the return from social media marketing.

The response rate of direct mail outpaces all digital channels and cost-competitive at approximately $19 cost-per-acquisition.

Direct marketing is not made equal and the formatting of the mail piece is a factor when it comes to the rate per response:

- Oversized envelopes   5% rate of response
- Postcards   4.25% rate of response
- Dimensional   4% rate of response

- Catalogs   3.9% rate of response
- Letter-sized envelopes   3.5% rate of response

Tracking where the leads come from or where they see your direct mail piece for the first time is the only downside to direct mailings. However, if you wish to track your direct mail, you can rent Post Office boxes and telephone numbers to track where the responses are coming from.

For example, you can open P.O. boxes in Fort Lauderdale and Palm Beach, FL at a UPS store in each area. Your direct mail piece has the address of each of the P.O. box locations and a separate telephone number for each. Check each box weekly to see if any responses have arrived.

The direct mail piece can be one that allows the recipient to write any information about a property they wished to sell and how to contact them.

There are fewer businesses are using direct mail to reach potential customers. This means that there is an opening for you to stand out and get attention for your mailer from the start. (Landau, 2019)

Diversify your rental property investments –

Diversifying your investments is another important way to grow your real estate rental business.

No one should put all their finances in one basket because that brings great risk. If it's all in one place, you can lose it all.

Real estate markets do frequently vary and if all your investments are in one kind of real estate or solely in one market, your finances will suffer when the market falls off.

If you diversify your investments, you spread your risk of losing it all.

When some investments fall off and are producing negative cash flow, other investments that are performing well will balance out the losses.

Having rental properties from various sectors performing well and generating positive cash flow, you can purchase more properties and grow your real estate investments faster.

Consider different locations to invest in and vary your real estate investment strategies.
To summarize, real estate investors who wish to grow and add to their real estate investment portfolio want to achieve financial independence.

These tips can help you grow your rental property business.
Of course, it takes focus, persistence, and hard work to gain increases in rental income, accumulate more properties and grow your real estate portfolio.

CHAPTER 5

How Today's Technology Can Keep You Informed

Technology Can Change Your Real Estate Business

Technology has infiltrated many industries and real estate is one of them. All participants –agents, home buyers, and home sellers – and it has been for the better.

As a real estate investor, the most challenging part of the business is how competitive the market is and how you need to employ every weapon that's available to build your business. Using new technology that is available is one of the best ways to do this.

The following are some of the ways real estate investors can boost their business by leveraging technology.

<u>Property Search</u> – When it comes to searching for properties, the Internet comes into play leveled the playing field.

In the past, it took an expert to determine when and where new properties became available, as well as figure out homes sales that were comparable for that specific area.

However, today, this information is instantaneous with a couple of clicks.

Finding For Sale properties is incredibly simple by using any credible real estate website. If you're looking FSBO (for sale by owner) properties Craigslist is a good website that can be fruitful and Auction.com is a good site for deals if you lean towards foreclosures.

As an investor, you can scale your portfolio using technology with free online education, the availability of sales comps, rental estimates and access to online deals, and simple ways to evaluate the deal.

Sales Comps Availability – Zillow is a great website for investors who are savvy and looking to work up CMAs in minutes.

Rental Estimates – Zillow has a ton of data and rental estimates are one of them. Zillow has rental estimates, particularly for single-family homes.

Another way to get updated rental estimate information is to call up a local property manager to check on rents.

Managing Leads – If you're still stuck on Post-It notes or using a notebook to jot down your leads, you're back in old school days. But if you want to grow your business and use technology to keep on top of the prospects then a CRM can fill the bill.

Direct Mail – If your strategy for marketing includes direct mail, this is another way to make use of a list provided by ListSource and upload a list to a mailing service.

A schedule can be developed to deliver in advance and are in line with your budget and goals. It gives you the chance to prod your targets regularly until they respond.

Improve Tenant Relationships and Asset Management

– Real estate investors can control online apartment management software making it possible for tenants to lease an apartment online, make deposits, pay rent and fees as well as submit maintenance requests all on one website.

Using technology enhances the experience of the tenants by making everything related to the property smooth and quick.
Real estate investors have found it possible to monitor their assets and everything going on across their portfolios.
They can keep track of expenses, working being done, or organizing property data.

Real estate rental technology is growing. If you're a real estate investor who perhaps owns one or two rental properties and still working your day job, or you're an investor who has been expanding your real estate business and has multiple rental properties, all of these properties need managing and maintaining at the highest level.
Hiring a property management company is probably the wisest way to go if you cannot manage your properties in the manner they need to be monitored. This component of ownership is vital.
Owning rental properties is one element of having a real estate business. The other factor is the tenants who are residing in those properties.

The income generated by tenants paying their rent keeps those properties solvent and running and keeping your tenants happy where they live.

How your assets are managed directly aligns with their value. You, as the owner and landlord, are responsible to have the properties maintained properly and according to laws instituted by the State, city, and municipality the properties are located.

Property management is the most important component of your investing undertakings. In order to serve landlords with ways to manage their properties that make it easier than ever before, a number of apps, startups, and platforms are cropping up to help this process.

Another reason to hire a property management company is to stay on top of the latest trends in the real estate industry.

They remain informed about the possible impact that economic trends can have on their business.

Staying prepared about what issues can, over time, come to pass, they are able to adapt themselves to any adverse circumstances and keep the best interests of their clients in mind while they work to protect their client's investments.

The Developing Property Management Terrain

Having your properties cared for by a property management company can assist you in growing your business. If you are considering doing so, this is a good time to research some property management firms and interview them. Once you choose one or two, discuss your needs and the rental properties that you own. (PMI Signature, 2017)

The property management company will give you their background and experience in the management of properties and the kinds they service, and they will also keep you informed about what trends are possibly facing investors and owners.

- **They recognize the significance of professional relationships** – Successful property management firms in the real estate industry are advancing those relationships to endure any financial tempests can menacing the industry as a whole.

- **They are up-to-date on the current trends** – As an investor and landlord, you need to be in the know as well. You can be kept aware of the latest information by researching and reading pertinent trade journals, and the business section of your local newspaper. As an example, the trend of increased evictions within urban areas that has been a continuing problem for landlords is one that could affect your rental property.

- <u>They will make a list of future potentials</u> - This is not about envisioning the future but getting ahead of your need's investor. They are envisioning adjustments in the area where your properties are located. In order to be proactive, make your own notes about any changes you are aware of the atmosphere regarding rentals and perform your own research in conjunction with them.

Recognize that there are numerous ways you, as a real estate investor, can have a beneficial relationship with a property management company and the important information they can provide can help your business grow and maintain its profitability. (PMI Signature, 2017)

The Necessity for Technology

In order to increase the value of your rental property is by offering technology that other property managers or landlords do not. Consider that consumers of today look for options and advantages that add value to a property, particularly when they are looking for a rental.

If you can satisfy a need and add value for your tenants, they may forgive any possible shortcomings that may happen in other areas.

Although technology can be expensive and your budget may not allow for everything on the following list, just by adding one may give you the ability to lessen any problems with your tenants.

In adding the technology a yet to come increase in rent can be justified by the addition. (Michael, 2017)

You can install the following to enhance the rentability of your property:

- Online tenant portal
- Home security system
- Smart home technology
- Wi-Fi service

Regardless of the significance and need for technology, keep in mind that most tenants would be ecstatic if there was a dishwasher to use.

Being a property manager or landlord is a difficult enough job. It's important to focus on the basics first and not allow the technology to make it all more complex.

Current Technologies Transforming Rental Property Management

Welcome to the world of Cloud-based property management software for the modern manager:

<u>AppFolio</u> – The largest company on this list, this SaaS property management service targeting mid-range to large property managers was launched in 2007.
Klaus Schauser, a former Entrepreneur of the Year founded AppFolio raised $30 million from private investors prior to going public in 2015 at $74.4 million. This indicates that the market has favorably responded to their service. <u>https://www.appfolio.com/</u>

<u>Pros</u> – AppFolio lets you roam across the range of property management including tenant screening, accounting or rent collection.

<u>Cons</u> – Not a good fit for a startup real estate investor, but great for larger property managers.

<u>Buildium</u> – Launched in 2004, this Boston-based company has become embedded in ample market share from conventional property managers, gaining 12,500 in 2016 by expanding in 46 countries worldwide and 1 million residential units.
Buildium has many of the same features as AppFolio – accounting to rent collection to tenant screening.
<u>https://learn.buildium.com/</u>

Pros – This is a high-end answer that actually fits an investor with a couple of properties, making room for future real estate tycoons.

Cons – It does fit the smaller investor, but it's still an expense that can be circumvented with 'do it yourself' tech solutions.
Or, you can use the next option···

Cozy – is the newest technology having launched in 2012. Looking to fill a gap in the property management software marketplace, independent landlords and small property management companies are the businesses Cozy targets.
https://cozy.co/

Pros - The company is designed to fill the void unmet by both AppFolio and Buildium. Cozy truly provides a greater answer for beginning investors and smaller landlords. It's designed to furnish the smaller investor with all the functionalities that the other two companies provide.

Cons – It has a payment option not enjoyed by everyone. However, the fee that a small investor pays is far less than the 10% to a property manager.
Visit all websites to get the latest information on pricing. (Michael, 2017)

Digital Files – More and more paper files and documents are becoming a thing of the past. It's more important today that you go digital.

Paper copies of rent checks, leases and vendor transactions can be lost. Creating a digital copy of all income, expenses and all transactions in your business, the worry about losing any paper copy or pages will be a thing of the past.
All of it will be on the digital record.

Organization is key in keeping good business records and keeping digital files makes it easier to do. You can sort all your documents when tax season hits. You can create varied folders for rental payments, expense transactions, and receipts for all of your rental properties.
Tech-enabled property management is one of the largest breakthroughs for the rental property industry.

CHAPTER 6

Managing Your Rental Property Finances

Your rental property investments have quite a bit of financial information that needs to be managed on a monthly basis.

This is imperative because, at tax time, you want to be able to report on each property you own both individually and combined.

As a real estate investor, you need to stay on top of many elements of your rental property finances to make sure the profitability and success of your investments are well-managed. Your properties need to be well-maintained and you need to have tenants who are dependable and responsible and your rental accounting needs continued attention.

It's imperative to keep precise financial records and keep track of your accounting. Owning rental properties brings quite a number of financial transactions to stay on top of.

Rental payments that are incoming in and money paid out for repairs, maintenance, mortgage payments (if the properties are financed), and if there is more than one property, all these finances become more complicated.

Having an accounting system that is right for your needs, keeping your finances in order can be easy.

Tax season will be easy, and your business will run effortlessly when you have your finances in order.

However, when your finances are not in order, costly mistakes can happen, bills to be paid may be overlooked incurring late fees, and possible problems with IRS can occur and they are a problem you don't want to have.

Keeping up with all of the finances of your rental property investments need to be sorted out and in control, so both your real estate investment business can function profitably.

Tips You Need to Manage Your Finances

SEPARATE YOUR PERSONAL AND BUSINESS ACCOUNTS

The best way to maintain all your finances is to keep your business accounts and personal accounts separate.

There are some rental property owners who frequently mix their business and personal finances because they feel it's more convenient for them to handle.

It's possible they don't have an accountant or a property manager handling their finances and they're managing their finances themselves.

Rather than having separate accounts for each of their properties and their personal finances, they pay everything out of one account and wait until tax time to separate which income and which payment was attached to which property and what personal bills of theirs were separate from everything else.

This is a huge mistake and conducting business in this way will only lead to bills falling through the cracks and difficulties at tax time. It's also a waste of time, but if you don't keep your business and personal accounts separated, you'll lose out on business and deductions that you could make, but don't and end up paying more towards taxes.

<u>Cash or Accrual Accounting</u> – Two ways you can manage your rental property investments are working with Cash accounting or Accrual accounting methods.

- <u>The Cash Accounting Method</u> – Until income is actually received, it is not counted. As an example, you wouldn't count any rental income from your tenants until they've paid you) and any expenses aren't counted until they're paid (a maintenance bill won't be counted as an expense until the bill is paid).

- <u>The Accrual Accounting</u> – All recorded financial transactions are made even when the cash has not actually been received. As an example, the rent from your tenants is due on the 1st of each month, but the payment is late and isn't paid until the 5th of the month. You still record the income of the rent as paid on the 1st of the month.

You can use either the cash or accrual accounting method, but once you begin to use one, stick with only that one. If you try to combine the two accounting systems and record some transactions using the cash accounting method and other transactions on an accrual basis, your financial books will become too confusing and harder to resolve and deal with come tax time. (Leap Property Management, 2019)

Both methods have pros and cons and if you're trying to decide which will work best for your rental properties, speak with a certified public accountant who specializes in rental property accounting.

Separate bank accounts for each of your rental properties –

Separate bank accounts for each of your rental properties is a must if you own multiple properties.

Using only one bank account for all your properties makes it harder to know which property's income and expenses are separate from another property.

Separating your financial accounts by each rental property will make it easier to see what income and expenses should be applied to each property.

The separation of accounts for each property also gives you a clear picture of which of the properties is the most profitable and if there is less profitability of another property tracking the reasons why is easier. All the income and expenses will be organized for you at tax time.

<u>Track expenses and income with a solid system</u> – Separate accounts for each rental property is important and taking it a step further, have a system to track expenses and income for all the properties as one that's solid and cohesive.

Rental property accounting software is available to keep your finances in order to make tracking your income and expenses easy, quick, and simple as covered in Chapter 5.

<u>Seasonal changes and large expenses</u> – Owning rental properties has its peaks and valleys financially.

Items such as appliances needing to be replaced or higher costs for maintenance in the winter. Regardless of how much you keep up with things, unexpected costs seem to arise unexpectedly.

If you don't plan for those large expenses and allow for them in your financial budget, they can throw your finances off, and sometimes not by a little, but a lot.

Don't let a situation that's expensive come up before you are to think about how you'll pay for it. Plan for these expenses so your finances are not impacted too heavily when they occur. (Leap Property Management, 2019)

Investment Property Analysis

You need to understand all the phrases used in real estate metrics so you can then understand all that goes into managing your rental property finances and developing an investment property analysis.

Real Estate Metrics

There are simple math formulas in real estate that help investors understand where they are in their business. Real estate metrics are specifically related to return on investment and financing. These metrics give investors the ability to analyze the real estate market as well as the analysis of investment property.

As a rental property investor, you must know the metrics used in real estate:

Net operating income (NOI) – Generated by the investment property, this is the rental income generated excluding all expenses and mortgage payments.

Cash Flow – The profit you derive from your rental property after all expenses are deducted. The cash flow is computed before tax income. This is a simple math equation – deduct all expenses from the total income to calculate the cash flow.

Capitalization rate – This is also known as the Cap Rate used to estimate if a property is worth the investment or not. This can also ascertain the sale price of a rental property.

The calculation to arrive at the cap rate is dividing the NOI by the property price at the time the property is purchased.

<u>Cash on cash return (CoC)</u> – This is a real estate metric that computes the return on every dollar invested in a property, which is another way to calculate your return on investment.

There are many other investment strategies and information that a rental property investor needs to acquire to understand the complexities of investing to become knowledgeable and successful. (Karani, 2019)

How to Develop an Investment Property Analysis

Being involved in the real estate world and buying rental investment properties can give you a great feeling of achieving your dream of growing a real estate investment business.

The possible glitch is locating the best properties.

Two kinds of data are what you should review to develop when analyzing a property - a Quantitative analysis and a Qualitative analysis.

<u>Quantitative data</u> – Investors can take many performance measures into consideration when they analyze real estate investments. In order to develop quantitative correctly, the focus is not on appreciation, but on the property returns and cash flow.

Income – You can calculate income in various ways. Cash Flow takes property payments into account. Net Operating Income doesn't take into account how the property is paid for.

Both the Cash Flow and Net Operating Income calculation styles are both helpful. Use Cash Flow if the payments and interest rates are known to the investor. Net Operating Income should be used to analyze the investment real estate if the payments and interest rates are unknown.

Cash Flow – The cash flow tells the profit generated by the property monthly or annually. This number is important because a break-even or negative cash flow points to the investor walking away from the property. Not a good deal.

In order to develop an analysis of an investment property is performing your due diligence and judging what rates are for investment costs, monthly expenses, and monthly income.

INVESTMENT COSTS

- Home Price – Paid cash or down payment towards the loan
- Closing costs – Approximately 6-7% of a loan
- Rehab – If necessary
- Inspection

MONTHLY EXPENDITURES

- Mortgage payment – Principal plus interest
- Property Tax

- Insurance
- HOA fees – If applicable
- Vacancies – 4-8% of rent
- Utilities – if the owner pays
- Property Management – 7-10% of the rent, if applicable
- Maintenance – 4-8%

MONTHLY REVENUE
- Rent the tenants are paying
- A possible property vacancy, assess a property nearby for its rental income and check with a property manager or realtor about approximately how much income you could expect once the property is rented
- For an investment property analysis, use the lower end of their estimates

CASH FLOW CALCULATION
- Monthly Revenue minus the Monthly Expenditures equal Cash Flow.

A way to pay down a 30-year mortgage over 18 years, add in one additional mortgage payment annually.
If you are investing in an Airbnb property, the costs that need to be included are fees for host service.

<u>NOI (net operating income)</u> – gives you the revenue for the property but excludes dollar amount that was paid for the property

- Add all revenue multiplied by 12 months. Annual Income equals the monthly revenue multiplied by 12 months

- Annual expenditures are reached by adding all expenditures and multiply by 12 months. Again, this does not include the monthly mortgage payment

- To reach the NOI subtract expenditures from revenue

- Annual expenditures minus Annual revenue = NOI

A decision can't really be made because this measurement is not enough. Analyzing multiple real estate investments at the same time is what this is more suited for.

RETURNS AND PROFITS

Returns can be analyzed in different ways. The first way is a formula that provides a return from the property.

Other methods aid to specify the importance of the returns.

<u>Return on Investment</u> – This is the revenue derived from the investment by arriving at the bottom line by accounting for all elements that affect it.

- The Cash Flow is reached by subtracting the known Revenue from the Monthly expenditures.

- The mortgage payment, which is principal plus interest is known. The mortgage's principal amount is the equity built on a monthly basis; The amount of money paid to purchase the property. Equity and cash flow are added.

- The annual return is reached by adding the Principal payment and Cash Flow together, then multiplying this figure by twelve months

- To reach the ROI (rate of investment) the Annual return needs to be divided by the total amount of investment.

<u>THE ROI AND CASH FLOW ARE THE MOST SIGNIFICANT METHODS IN DECIDING INVESTMENT ANALYSIS.</u>

If an investor doesn't identify what they are looking for, making calculations using all the formulas to reach the numbers are meaningless.

Here are more numbers to look at when coming to conclusions about your investment:

<u>Capitalization Rate (CAP)</u> – This number gives you the returns of the property that is separate from the financing.
This number is important because it is the way to understand the returns from the property without how the property is financed.

- The information it gives you is the return on the property as if the mortgage has been paid off.

- Cap Rate = NOI/Property price

- Property has a good cap rate depending on its locality. Rates range between 8%-12%. As the minimum goal in an area set the cap rate as average.

<u>CoC (cash-on-cash return)</u> – This is based on the total cash invested in the property.

- CoC = NOI divided by investment costs

- General good cash on cash return is 10%. However, this is depending on the location, the kind of property it is and the rental strategy.

COC - PRE-TAX CASH FLOW ANNUALLY/ INVESTMENT COSTS

- **Annual Pre-Tax Cash Flow** - is how much money that is left every month multiplied by 12 months. The equation is this:

- **Income minus Expenses = Pre-Tax Cash Flow**

- **Investment Costs** – This is how much cash you paid for the property

- **Monthly Pre-Tax Cash Flow x 12 Months = Annual Pre-Tax Cash Flow**

All the different calculations to evaluate a property can be daunting but they are major ones that should be looked upon as well as other costs that can aid in making comparisons of properties.
These calculations are beneficial by signifying average ranges. The location of the property impacts its performance.

Remember that when you are conducting investment analysis, the rates are the most recent costs, but vary annually.
For example, rents and rates probably will rise each year.
This means the calculations won't remain the same throughout the life of the investment.

When calculating Returns, another element to consider is Appreciation, although it is not a guarantee.

All this information takes into account the quantitative end of an investment property analysis.

The next part of an investment property analysis is qualitative information.

QUALITATIVE DATA

Rental Market – Check if a market is growing when you choose a market or an area. Lots of construction?

That indicates that housing is being built and people are moving into the area and bring tenants.

Another factor of an area is the job market because people go where the opportunities for jobs are available.

A low unemployment rate in a market is favorable.

Don't choose a market that has only one job industry as the dominant employer. The danger is that if the industry goes belly up and fails, the job market for the area is virtually killed and the ripple effect of a layoff is devastating for all parties.

<u>Neighborhood</u> – Make sure when you choose a neighborhood that the location is one that will draw tenants.

Be aware of what tenants are looking for and what sways them to rent in a neighborhood.

Schools, crime, transportation, amenities, noise, and zoning are factors for an investor to consider.

<u>Properties</u> – Get an inspection and appraisal!

These inspections are crucial for an investor to have performed on a property.   Knowing what the possible deal-breakers are after a property has been inspected.   You can stay the course with your budget that is set, and you don't want to invest in a property that will overtake your budget because of repairs both obvious and hidden.

All these criteria of the market, neighborhood and the property should be carefully considered and should also be a compliment with the cash flow budget.

Evaluating rentals to invest in takes quite a bit of calculating and research, yet it is rewarding to find an investment worth the work as well as get an education about different properties and markets as well.

<u>Predictive Analytics</u> – This term may sound very complex, predictive analytics is a concept is not difficult to understand. This analysis is a way of analyzing big data.   It uses past data to forecast future trends.   It is the center of data science where patterns are not identified even by experts.

Predictive analytics is not equal to fortunetelling, it can come pretty close.   Such analytics can be very useful because it creates a forecast that is reliable for what may happen in the future by including "the possible" situations and taking into account issues of risk.

Analytics and Real Estate Markets – Real estate markets are always changing, can be complex and, at a time, unstable. Real estate investors want the ability to assess whether a potential property will be a good one to invest in. They want to make informed decisions when they make an investment in order to maximize their return.

Predictive analytics gives investors the ability to evaluate where and when to invest objectively, optimize their choices and decide the true value of properties.

Market cycle risks, price forecasts and attraction analytics are additional metrics that are key to investors.

Trends – Predictive analytics can give real estate investors with numerous benefits when it comes to trends, culminating in important operational effectiveness and cost savings that are mainly predicated on precise, real-time predictions.

Investors can quickly decide which are valuable investments, anticipating neighborhood and predictive maintenance that will make for a greater marketing return on investments in the future and a better-informed investor.

When an investor is considering buying an investment property, recognizing the trends is vital because these analytics evaluate the home values and risks of the future for an investor, generating red and green markers that will specify whether a potential property investment should or should not be purchased.

<u>Purchasing the best properties</u> – Predictive analytics gives real estate investors to possibly forecast the top property design as a future purchase, determining what's trendy and what isn't.

Investors want to derive the most from their money so if the demand for rentals is leaning towards young families, an investor won't have to buy a massive investment property to aim the young family. To target this type of tenant, a two-bedroom home would be enough.

By using this type of analytics, an investor is describing the home characteristics that are wanted and in demand, generating the most return on investment for the investor.

CHAPTER 7

Your Responsibilities and Legal Rights

As an investor, you are investing in properties, analyzing new markets, and running an investment business.

However, you are not just a rental property investor, you are also a landlord. Although your main focus is on investing in real estate and now growing your real estate investment business, another focus that is just as important as being a landlord and knowing all the rules, regulations, responsibilities, and legal rights that come along with that mantle.

You may think the cases that come before Judge Marilyn Milian on the People's Court and Judge Judy on her program are contrived for entertainment but they're not. The litigants and the cases are real and are arbitrated to resolution.

You learn quite a bit about landlord and tenant actions and how they are treated in a court of law. These two examples of cases involving landlords and their tenants where one landlord acted without knowledge of a tenant-landlord law and the other out for neglecting her tenants.

Landlord #1 who owns a single-family rental in New Jersey found out that he could be liable to pay a former tenant twice the amount of security deposit she felt he owed her.

The tenant's security deposit of $2,175. She needed to move out because the monthly rent of $1,425 was too overwhelming for her as a single mother and she could no longer live in the home due to her divorce.

The tenant spoke to the landlord, explained her predicament, and told him that she needed to leave a month before her lease was up. She hadn't given him a 30-day notice. The landlord thought notice had to be given in 90 days before vacating.

The landlord asked if she could stay to the end of October, when her lease ended, but could not. She said she could no longer afford it. She told him to use the security deposit for the $1,425 for the last month's rent and return the remaining $750 to her. She left on September 30th and moved in with herself and her child to her mother's place of residence.
The landlord only returned $590 of the remaining deposit. The tenant had not cashed the check but instead filed a lawsuit for the remaining $160.

Fast forward to what was resolved: The landlord thought 90 days was how much notice he needed for the tenant to give. New Jersey State law states 30 days' notice is required from a tenant to inform a landlord of vacating the premises.
The landlord deducted for spackling and retouching the paint for $160.

He was asked how many holes had to be spackled and he claimed 500 in three rooms. The judge asked for proof. The landlord produced photos. She asked how much it cost him to have the holes filled. He said he did them himself, but the supplies and paint were purchased to do the job. The landlord had receipts for those items.

The judge said the spackling and retouching paint job would be left at the $160 deduction.

The last thing that the judge let the landlord know was that he should review New Jersey's tenant-landlord laws to be clear on when a tenant needs to inform him of when they will be vacating the property and about how he handled the letter of explanation and the return of the remaining security deposit to the tenant after she moved out.

He had not sent the letter within the 30 days period as defined by law, and because the letter was late, the tenant could actually be awarded twice the amount of money according to New Jersey State law.

The landlord thought did not know this either. Fortunately for him, the tenant didn't know that either.

The judge reiterated what both parties did in this situation and fortunately for the landlord, the tenant had received what was due to her. The security deposit of $2,175 minus $1,425 and the $160 for repairs was a total of $1,585. The total remaining of $590 was given to the tenant.

Since the tenant already had the check in the amount of $590, the judge ruled in favor of the defendant. The tenant said she would not pursue filing for double the amount and just wanted the case to be over.

The case was settled, the tenant was satisfied and the landlord left with better education about being a landlord than before he walked into the courtroom.

Landlord #2 was being sued by a married couple with two children who resided in the landlord's property, a single-family home. The couple was suing for their December and January rent to be returned to them due to no heat or hot water during those months because the hot water heater wasn't working. This was during a pretty frigid winter in New York City.

They also wanted to be reimbursed for their hotel bill.

They had to move into a hotel until the problem was resolved.

The tenants were paying $2,200 a month. The judge questioned the plaintiffs about what they did to contact the landlord and let her know about the problem with the hot water heater.

The landlord had been out of town from December 2018 through February 2019. The tenants sent text messages and called and spoke with her on the phone. The landlord stated that she had called to get someone in to check the problem with the hot water heater.

The landlord relayed this information to the tenants and told them what day and time this was to happen. That day came and went and no one showed up to check the water heater.

The tenants called again to complain about the problem and were beginning to get the feeling that the landlord felt "bothered and annoyed" about being called. The landlord stated she called the same company again and the same thing happened – they didn't show up.

The family finally left and stayed in a hotel until the water heater problem was resolved in mid-January.

The judge then questioned the landlord and asked why it had taken so long to get this hot water heater repaired or replaced. The landlord seemed a bit too casual about the problem.

Her defense is that she tried to get someone to go out to the property to have it fixed, but she was out of town so she really couldn't do very much.

Huge mistake on the part of the landlord. What was happening to her tenants was they were being denied the **warranty of habitability**. The fact that her tenants were living without heat and hot water because of her negligence and lack of urgency was inexcusable and unacceptable to the judge.

The judge felt the attitude of the landlord was too cavalier for a situation that was a health issue as well as a habitability issue.

The tenants were awarded their full month's rent for December and half of January's rent because the problem was remedied in mid-January. She also awarded them their hotel stay at $75 per day for 10 days, $750.

In total, the judgment was $4,050 to the plaintiff.

Obviously, the landlord did not have a reliable network of contractors or handymen who could have checked to see what the problem was and either repaired the hot water heater or replaced it. Now, on top of replacing the hot water heater, the landlord was to pay her tenants for their extreme discomfort.

Landlord Responsibilities

A landlord wears many different hats and each has its own distinctive set of responsibilities that a landlord should be knowledgeable about.

A landlord needs to be aware of their responsibilities before you invest in rental properties and self-manage them.

What are the responsibilities of a landlord –

The responsibilities of a landlord include the duty to a tenant to guarantee and assurance of livability assuring the rental is clean, safe, and able to be lived in without detriment to your tenant.

Landlords have a responsibility to pay the property taxes, maintain the property as well as utilities. They must also comply and are responsible to abide by all rules mandated by local, state, and federal laws.

Responsibilities of a landlord to their tenants –

Regardless of the type of lease in place with a tenant (annual or month-to-month) a safe and clean place to live. A tenant has a right to have a safe and clean home.

The rental has to have working heat and hot water.

An infestation of pests such as mice or roaches or a broken lock on the building's front door are breaches of the warranty of habitability.

The livability and quality of the rental is the inherent right and is a statement that covers all aspects of a functioning home.

A landlord needs to provide for additional factors and not just the warranty of habitability.

Stay up-to-date with all codes - Different codes will apply based on the city and state property is located. All properties that are rentals must comply with these codes.

Lead Paint – Any property built pre-1978, obliges a landlord to submit a lead paint disclosure form to tenants. The lead paint booklet explains lead paint used in buildings that were built before 1978 and what the risks are concerning lead paint.

Mold – A water build-up or leak can create a mold situation in a rental property whether it's an apartment or a single-family home. If mold is found in a rental property by law, a landlord is must rid the mold from the area that it is affecting the property.

A couple renting a single-family home in Florida noticed that the heavy rainstorms were leaking into the house via the roof.

The couple complained to the landlord who sent someone to "patch" the roof. This was ongoing each time it rained and the landlord made no move to have the roof replaced.

Finally, after another downpour of rain, water was coming in through an overhead light fixture. This was alarming as it could create a serious electrical situation.

The landlord called a roofer to do another "patch" job.

The roofer stated after inspecting the roof that he would not sacrifice his twenty-year license on just patching the roof.

The roof needed to be replaced.

The landlord also called an electrician to check on the wiring that had been affected by the rainstorm. The electrician informed the landlord that the wiring was damp and the insulation surrounding the wiring needed to be replaced because it had deteriorated because of mold eating away and leaving that entire area exposed with no insulation.

The electrician went on to state that this situation had been going on for some time because of the leaks in the roof.

In all, aside from the $6,000 to replace the roof, the landlord had to pay $2,500 more to re-insulate the area that surrounded the wiring as well as having the area where the rain leaked in rewired as well. The area was not a large one, but enough to make a significant dent in this landlord's budget.

Fortunately, the problem didn't extend to other parts of the crawl space, but what was found was sufficient and could have begun to affect other areas of insulation.

So much for patching a leaky roof.

<u>Standards of Occupancy</u> – Each rental will vary on occupancy standards. Each state has a code that will defend the occupancy standard. New York State's occupancy standard is described as in a bedroom of 70 square feet one person with an additional person, it is 50 square feet.

Counted towards rooms of occupancy are living rooms and dining rooms.

Learn and understand your local occupancy standards to comprehend what the maximum amount of people can reside in the rental. Be cautious of discriminating if a large family applies for a smaller rental.

<u>The installation of Smoke and Carbon Monoxide Detectors</u> – Every state dictates by law the mandatory amount of smoke and carbon monoxide detectors for every room and floor of the property. The number of detectors may vary on what the state law orders, or if any appliances are in a room.

Make sure that all detectors are supplied with new batteries when a new tenant moves in. This will alleviate guessing when the batteries were last changed.
Research the laws where the property is located and what specific laws apply.

<u>Safety in the Common Areas</u> – Common areas such as garages, hallways, and laundry rooms need to be kept clear and free of any dangers or hazards. This is the responsibility of the landlord who owns a multi-level property.
Replacing light bulbs that have blown out and handrails for the stairwells are included in common areas.

<u>Window Guard installation</u> – Window guards must be installed when requested, in writing, by any tenant living in an apartment who has any children 10 years old or younger.
This would cover children living in the property regularly, or any children who spend a lot of time in the property.

<u>Weather-Related Laws</u> – If you own a property in a city that has a good amount of snowfalls in the winter, both the tenant and the landlord are obliged to ensure the sidewalk in front of the property is clear and free of snow and ice.

In the event anyone injures themselves by slipping and falling on the portion of the sidewalk in front of the property, both the landlord and the tenant share equally in the responsibility for any damages.

Read your state and local laws to be sure of all legal information.

Landlords and Rental Responsibilities

You're a business owner as a landlord. Your clients are your tenants and the rental property is an asset.

To protect your investment you're living up to your responsibility as a landlord.

The repairs, accounting, and expenditures are done correctly, keeping the landlord honest, complying with the laws.

<u>Property Maintenance</u> – There are varying laws that every town or city has regarding property standards.

Care of the property's lawn and trash are all factors scrutinized by your municipality.   Allowing an accumulation of trash, or disrespecting parking rules only creates problems with law enforcement and possibly the neighbors.

Everyone is subject to these laws and you should maintain your property accordingly

<u>Repairs</u> - At the beginning of the chapter, it stated that the occupants of the rental are entitled to have a guarantee of a safe and clean home. That being said, the upkeep of repairs for the rental property needs to be addressed by the landlord.
Clogged drains, peeling paint, clogged gutters, dripping faucets all need to be fixed. Keeping up on the repairs is also a way of protecting your rental property.

An example of a problem getting out of hand are gutters that are clogged and having water accumulating near the base of the house can create a basement that is wet and the increased moisture that can cause harmful mold in the property.

Other maintenance needs are to have all functions of the property running effectively, such as heat as well as a cooling system. Either of these not performing well during winter and summer months present a health danger to your tenants

Stay on top of repairs so issues don't get out of hand and costly.

Legal Responsibilities of the Landlord

Landlords should be aware of the Fair Housing Act and the Fair Credit Reporting Act. The tenant selection process is what these acts regulate to make sure it is done fairly and accurately.

Fair Housing Act (FHA) – Landlords use tenant screening as a process to find tenants that are suitable to rent their rental property.   This can create a problem when discriminatory procedures are used to screen tenants.

The Civil Rights Act was enacted and signed on April 11, 1968, and the Fair Housing Act of 1968 is Title VIII of the Civil Rights Act.

The Fair Housing Act forbade discrimination based on national origin, race, religion, sex, family status and handicap regarding the renting, sale, and loans for purchasing a home. Read more at the Housing and Urban Development site, www.HUD.gov.

Landlords were included in this Act by the U.S. Government due to their capability of shaping neighborhoods' diversity. It is vital that there be no discrimination by landlords in their decisions of who they will choose as a renter.

Single renters preferred and "Looking for Female Renters" are listings that are commonly seen when a landlord is looking for a certain type of renter.

Screening practices should be free of discrimination and it is a landlord's responsibility to accept and follow the laws instituted by the FHA

Complying with FCA (Fair Credit Reporting Act) –

This Act applies to the process of collecting sensitive seem related to landlords.   However, when you're and private information with regards to a tenant application, the responsibility to handle the information correctly is the responsibility of the landlord or someone designated by the landlord to collect the information.

It is imperative that rental applications are kept in a secure location. Also, written, signed consent from the potential tenant is needed to run a background check. This can be added to the tenant application. Signed consent is also needed if you want to get in touch with a tenant's employer or former landlord.
Do not share details of a potential tenant's information with others.

A landlord is obliged to send a notice to an applicant who has been denied occupancy of the rental. The applicant can request a free report from the consumer reporting agency used to check their background.

<u>Legal Responsibility to Neighbors</u> - The actions of a tenant, if it interferes with a neighbor's comfortable enjoyment of their home and property, is the responsibility of the landlord.
Noise issues, criminal activity, and drug dealing are the types of problems that can disturb a neighbor living adjacent to the landlord's rental property. Some cities hold the landlord accountable are they are fined for any infractions.

Check the town or city the hours of noise ordinances where your rental is located.
You can include this in your lease in order to avoid any issues. You will have a way of resolving the issue with your tenant.

An example is if you receive a complaint from a neighbor, contact your tenant to get their side of the issue. If you receive another complaint after the first one is resolved, you can either give a second warning or, depending on how well these tenants behave overall, ask them to vacate.

A landlord should make it their business to know the neighbors. There are some landlords who give their contact information in case of an emergency or if any issues arise with the rental property.

This is a way of being kept abreast of any issues by a neighbor. They also can contact you first before they file a complaint with the municipality.

Right to Enter – The right to privacy is the right of an occupant as a renter. For this reason, states designate laws regarding rights to enter by a landlord.

- Entering rented premises can only be done because of the following;

- Making repairs or assessing the need for repairs in the event of an emergency;

- To show prospective new renters or owners the property – this needs to be done with at least 24-48 hours' notice as a courtesy to the tenant;

- Entering the property, in most states, the landlord must let the tenant know they will be entering the property. However, check with your state or local ordinances to make sure how much notice is needed to be given.

<u>Non-Renewal a Lease</u> – States have varied rules regarding the renewal of leases.

Normally, a landlord should notify a tenant 60 days prior to their lease ending if you will be renewing it or not. This will allow the tenant time to look for another rental.

<u>Pet Deposits/Emotional Support Animals</u> –

The allowances for emotional support animals are on the rise between landlords and tenants.

As a landlord, it's vital to differentiate the difference between an emotional support animal and a pet.

Currently, almost any animal can be designated as a support animal. A hamster, cockatiel, cat or dog and many other animals fall into this category. The animal gives its owner emotional support.

The No Pet Policy cannot be applied to emotional support and service animals. Service animals are professionally trained dogs, while an ESA usually hasn't been professionally trained.

There are some renters who have an online health professional give their pet a designation as an ESA.

It is illegal to charge a tenant a pet deposit if an animal has an ESA designation. A landlord must accommodate this animal.

You will expose yourself to liability if you deny someone the opportunity to rent your property based on a support animal.

<u>Hotel expenses</u> – As a landlord, you are responsible to offer a rental property that has acceptable water, electricity, heating, and a sound structure.

There are times that situations come about that cause a rental until to be uninhabitable for a time.

Typically this is caused by the need to have repairs done, unexpected disasters or major problems with the property.

While the rental is uninhabitable and your tenants have to vacate until repairs are completed.

When this happens, what responsibility does the landlord have in covering the hotel bills?

When do tenants obtain hotel bills? – If a fire, electrical short, termites, leaky pipe or other emergencies that are unexpected that make the rental uninhabitable, the tenants have to move out until the problem is resolved.

Usually, tenants will live in a hotel while the damages are fixed. Tenants are sometimes under the impression the landlord should pay for their hotel stay and erroneously think the homeowner's policy of their landlord will compensate for the cost of the hotel.

Or, they presume that they will immediately check-in and stay in a hotel they choose and the bill will be paid by the landlord.

The tenant's beliefs are incorrect. This frequently leads to disagreements.

The landlord's insurance policy does not cover costs for a tenant's relocation as well as it will not cover any damage to the tenant's belongings.

If the tenant carries renter's insurance, both hotel stays and property damage and loss will be covered.

Most states will allow a tenant the ability to move from the rental without being penalized should their rental becomes not fit to live in for a lengthy period of time and there was no fault of the tenant for this happening.

The landlord will also have to prorate any rent that has been paid. Other laws will go into effect if the fault for any damage falls on the tenant.

In order to be clear about the relocation of a tenant in the event the rental becomes damaged and uninhabitable, the lease should have it outlined as to what the landlord is responsible for and what the tenant should do in order to cover themselves.

A landlord is not bound to pay for hotel bills when their tenant needs to relocate because of unexpected repairs or damage that is out of the landlord's control.

The lease should have a clause added in the event of damage caused by the tenant that necessitates the property to be vacated for a period of time. It should also include point out how the rent will be addressed during the time the property cannot be lived in.

An unlivable rental property that needs to be vacated can probably have the rent prorated for the number of days the tenants could not occupy the property. In the interim, the tenants will pay for their own housing.

Any problem that arises because of negligence by the landlord for what he did or did not do, tenants can file a petition in small claims court to be reimbursed for their housing.

If a landlord schedules an inspection or fumigation or a remodeling that will take no more than 2-3 days, they may feel it is reasonable to pay for hotel costs because the tenants are good tenants and they would like to accommodate them.

State Responsibilities

There are state laws that are exclusive and apply to tenants and landlords. These laws are what a landlord needs to be aware of when you research state, city, and municipal laws:

Security Deposit – A range from 1 to 2.5 months' rent.

Security Deposit interest – Placing the deposit in a bank account that is an interest-bearing account. Some states require giving interest to the tenant.

Separate Security Deposit Account – Check to see if your State allows a landlord to intermingle security deposit funds with personal assets.

Return of Deposit deadline – Some cases have no statute. However, the time allotted varies anywhere from 14 to 45 days. State, city, and municipal laws should be checked for the time affecting your property.

Any additional fees and Pet Deposits – No fees are permitted that that include pet deposits. Check the law in the state the property is situated.

Rent Increase – Check you State's laws regarding rent increases before you do.

<u>Late Charges</u> – There are states that do allow an extension for rent to be paid while other States do not address the issue at all.

<u>Returned Check Fee</u> – Read the State laws where the rental is located if the tenant bounces a check and before you charge them a fee.

<u>Move-Out Inspection</u> – You, or a representative for you, need to do a move-out inspection. Do you do it before the tenant has totally moved all their belongings, or after when the rental property is totally vacated?   Understand the timelines of when to do an inspection.

<u>Eviction for Nonpayment</u> – Depending on the State, a notice of eviction can differ from 3-30 days.

<u>Required Notice prior to Entry</u> – This usually ranges from no notice to an obligatory notice.

<u>Emergency Entry - No notice</u> – Learn about your rights in case of an emergency entry is necessary.

<u>Small Claims Court</u>– A cap on financial claims in small claims court compensation if damage has occurred by the tenant of your rental property.
Again, check with your state laws regarding this.
Landlord responsibilities are numerous and the amount of work involved to manage and maintain your property can be daunting. However, your property is your asset and generates the passive income that you worked hard to earn.

Learn the laws of where properties are located, be cautious with any out of state property laws. You will become one of the most important components of your rental property business – a great landlord!

CHAPTER 8

Handling Your Bookkeeping and Taxes

The accounting of all the finances attached to your rental properties is crucial to maintain. Many real estate investors have their finances reviewed on a monthly basis to keep precisely kept accounts.

The importance of keeping the rental property accounts up-to-date with all receipts and notations regarding all the activities attached to each property cannot be stressed enough.

All income, expenses, repairs, renovations, and any purchases for a property must be noted along with receipts for proof of service or purchase.

In addition to the income and expenses of the property, any work is done by independent contractors, whether it be a part-time bookkeeper, roofer, handyman, etc., tax documents need to be filled out and signed. This is for any work that you pay out to the contractor that adds up annually to more than $600.

For example, you send out mailers seeking leads for properties that may be available for purchase to turn into rentals. You hire two people, who are independent contractors, also considered non-employees of your investment business.

You have both parties fill out a W-9.

Their job is to take your investor letter, fold, insert into envelopes, address, and stamp the envelopes.

After they complete the number of mailers, they take them to the post office to have them mailed.

Both people are paid $12 per hour. The work was done over 2.5 days working 8 hours per day and making a total of $240 over this time.

You send out different investor letters each month to different areas and each time the independent contractors work approximately the same amount hours.

At the end of the year, the two contractors have made $2,880 each. They should then be issued by you 1099. It is up to these contractors to report their earnings to the IRS by filing a personal 1040 form.

The following are explanations of each form and the penalties for a business owner not filing 1099 for an independent contractor

1099s and W-9s – These are tax documents that are important if you have work done on your rental properties by independent contractors. Understand what these documents are and how they should be used.

The contractor's **taxpayer ID is requested by a W-9 form**. This informs your accountant or tax professional about what kind of business they are (partnership or sole proprietor) and whether they need 1099 to file with the IRS.

1099 is the tax form that a non-employees income

(the non-employee being the contractor) from the work on the rental property business for any given year. This also applies to anyone who works for you in connection with your real estate investment business.

This is the form needed for the contractor or other non-employees to file their taxes, reporting the income they received working for you.

1099 is needed only if a non-employee was paid more than $600 during the year.

Every non-employee who does work for you needs to fill a W-9 as soon as you begin working with them. If you pay them beyond $600 in the calendar year, 1099 must be issued by you and sent to the non-employee by January 31st of the next year.

These forms are essential for your tax filing. You need to make sure all the proper documents are in order when tax time rolls around. Penalties for not filing 1099 tax forms are costly. Speak with a tax professional to check that you have everything correct before you file.

To give you an idea of the penalties for not filing the correct information is:

There is a $50 fine for each 1099 that is filed within 30 days of the due date and $191,000 as a maximum penalty.

If the filing is 30 days after the August 1st due date, the penalty is $100 per 1099 and $547,000 as a maximum penalty. (efile4biz.com, 2019)

Needless to say, filing 1099s for all those non-employees who do work for you is really important and nothing to do haphazardly. It can be an expensive detriment to your finances if you don't follow the correct process to file them properly. (Leap Property Management, 2019)

Mortgage, Insurance and Property Taxes

<u>Mortgage Payment</u> – Although this is a responsibility that's a given, it is worth pointing out.

A "legal agreement by which a building society, bank, etc., is the definition of a mortgage and lends money at interest in exchange for taking the title of the debtor's property, with the condition that the conveyance of title becomes void upon the payment of the debt" per the Oxford Dictionary. (Worral, 2018) Late fees will be incurred if you miss one mortgage payment against your mortgage agreement. The bank will probably not foreclose on your property if you miss one payment.

However, if you are past due 60 days on your mortgage, the late payments will be reported to the credit bureaus and will have an effect on your credit score in a negative manner.

You will technically be in default if you are late paying your mortgage more than 90 days – even if it's the 91st day.

A letter will be sent from your lender that the loan is in arrears and the loan will fall into default.

The lender will foreclose on the property unless the arrears are paid in full within the 90 days.

Maintain Your Insurance – Proof of insurance is required before a lender will provide you with a rental property loan. Some lenders will set up an escrow account that pays your insurance policy.

In order to protect your tenant's property, requiring your tenants to purchase renter's insurance is a good idea.

A renter's insurance policy covers the tenant's belongings that do not get covered by the homeowner's policy of the landlord. The monthly cost runs approximately $5 to $15 monthly.

Have a renter's insurance policy as a stipulation in the lease.

Other notable insurance includes water, fire, and flood coverage.

Create an LLC or invest in an Umbrella insurance policy – There are other ways to further protect your rental investment. This can be done by setting up an LLC or by purchasing an Umbrella policy.

LLC (Limited Liability Company) – is a legal entity that permits investors to purchase and own real estate in a manner that protects them from personal liability. The investor buys and sells real estate as well as handle other business in the name of the LLC, not with the investor as an individual.

The purpose to do business in this way is all business is done through the LLC and not you personally.

Umbrella Insurance Policy – This is a category of personal life insurance. This type of insurance can be essential, especially if you become liable for a claim that is larger than either your auto insurance or homeowner's insurance to cover the claim.

An additional liability insurance layer is offered by an umbrella policy insurance for your properties and covers between $1 million to $5 million dollars in damage.

<u>Pay Your Utilities</u> - The lease between landlord and tenant will decide what utilities are the responsibility of the landlord and which are the utilities a tenant pays for.

Your rental property can be foreclosed for unpaid taxes and fees by the city or town where your property is located.

In January, for example, in some cities, a tax foreclosure list is available.

Fees and taxes that can be owed are user fees, garbage service, and property taxes.

Owners must pay foreclosure fees if their property appears on the tax foreclosure list when a judgment is given.

Landlords will pay for water and trash pickup.

The potential of having your rental property foreclosed for non-payment of a bill will have you think twice of allowing the utility bill to be in your tenant's name.

<u>Create Landlord Utility accounts</u> – Many of the utility companies offer landlords connection service. These accounts offer some advantages:

You have the ability to tell if the tenant has had the utilities for the rental put in their name and has had your name removed.

When there is tenant turnover you can have the utilities reverted back to your name, allowing for the rental to continue having electricity, water, and heat instead of waiting to have all the utilities hooked up again.

<u>**Responsibilities with Security Deposits**</u> – Most landlords do not know what laws are in place with regards to how the security deposit for a tenancy should be handled.

Due to this lack of knowledge, it's important to deposit the security deposit money into an escrow account and learn how to open one.

One of the most usual mistakes made with security deposit funds is the co-mingling the funds within the same account with other money.

You can learn more about the security deposit laws in each state by going to:
https://www.nolo.com/

To learn how to open an escrow account go to:
<u>https://www.rentprep.com/landlord-tips/escrow-account-security-deposit/</u>

This is what can happen to a landlord because they did not handle their security deposits properly:

Consider a landlord rented their rental property to a couple and when they vacated, they destroyed the property.

Damages made by the tenant that was beyond a security deposit made beyond the scope of the deposit that was more than how much a security deposit covered.

Unfortunately, the way the security deposit was handled improperly. The security deposit, according to State law, was to be kept in a separate interest-bearing account and not with any other funds or accounts.

The law also stated the tenants were to be given information as to what bank the deposit was being held. The landlord did not follow the State laws and forfeited the security deposit.

There are 23 States that have specific rules on the handling of the security deposit.

Whether your state requires it or not, it's a good practice to keep the security deposit funds in separate accounts.

Make sure you follow your State's rules so you can retain security funds if there is damage to one of your rental properties.

Upfront Fees – Landlords are inclined to be cautious about their liabilities by charging upfront fees to tenants:

- Application fees
- Security deposit
- First month's rent
- Last month's rent

Each State regulates these fees.

For example, in Massachusetts charging upfront application fees is illegal.

State's also set the limits to what can be charged for security deposits.

Hire a Certified Public Accountant (CPA) – If you own one rental property and you have a knack with math then it's probably better to handle your finances on your own.

However, owning multiple properties, or math was your worst subject, you should seriously consider hiring a CPA especially one that has specific experience with rental property investing.

A CPA should have the ability to manage the properties, the income, and expenses, be knowledgeable of how to maximize your tax benefits and keep the business and its finances running smoothly as you grow your business.

As you add more rental properties to your business, your finances will grow more complex and it is why you need the support of a CPA. This will ensure that when tax time rolls around, you're not panicking and losing sleep over how they'll get done.

Hiring a CPA is an investment. They're an investment that, in the long run, pays for itself. Consider the energy, time, and money they save you.

They're managing your finances freeing you to focus on the real estate investment end of your business, conducting CMAs on the next potential property to expand your real estate portfolio.

<u>Prepare your tax documents early</u> – Waiting until the last minute to get started on preparing your taxes is probably the worst thing you can do.

Long before April 15th. you should be getting together with your CPA to review your finances and prepare your taxes.

The process will be more stressful and leaves an opening for something to get overlooked which could cost you money.

The overlooked item could either have benefited you by including it in your tax return and cost you because you didn't, or it will hurt you if there is a review of your tax return and it shows an amount of money still owed to the government.

Either way, it's a financial loss that could have been avoided. Begin working on your taxes early.

Familiarize yourself with the IRS website - Most people would rather not access the IRS website, but actually, it is a fountain of information especially a section that devotes itself to rental real estate and federal tax responsibilities.

As an example, the IRS lays out how you need to report the rental income. You may think that's pretty obvious, but some real estate investors who go it alone without the help of a CPA or who are new to the rental property investing don't know the nuances that the IRS deems rental income. (IRS, 2019)

For example, if you receive advance rent in any amount prior to the period it covers, that amount of advance rent must be reported.

In other words, if you sign a lease for ten years, the rent will be $5,000 the first year that you receive as income and the rent of $5,000 the final year.

The IRS considers the rent for the last year as advance rent and mandates that the income of $10,000 to be reported as the revenue in the first year as well.

Additionally, the IRS considers security deposits as rent in advance and should be included in the income when you receive it.

There is an interesting twist to the security deposit rule – don't include it as revenue if it will be paid back in full to the tenant when the tenancy ends.

However, a portion or all of the security deposit is retained due to the tenant breaching the terms of the lease, you must include the security deposit funds as income in that year.

Another example is a tenant making a payment to cancel their lease. This is considered rent and should be included in your income the year it was received.

If you trade the amount of monthly rent for a service your tenant can provide you, you must report is as revenue.
If your tenant offers to paint the rental in lieu of paying two months' rent, the amount of the two months' rent is considered rent and must be reported as income. (IRS, 2019)

The IRS answers many of the questions a real estate investor ask regarding their rental properties.
Along with information on what the IRS considers income, they outline what deductions are allowable, how to report rental income and expenses and the records that you should keep relating to all your rental properties. They give good tips.

Managing rental investment finances is an immense job.
It demands time, attention and accuracy to manage the finances attached to each of your rental properties and your business overall.

Whether you're going it alone or already have a CPA handling your rental property business, keep informed about your finances, request a monthly accounting, and file your taxes on time to avoid penalties and problems.

CHAPTER 9

Dealing with Unexpected Rental Expenses

Dealing with rental properties has its ups and downs.

There will be periods when everything seems to be running smoothly, with no headaches or complaints and then BAM! you get a call that there's a leak in the roof of your single-family rental and another call comes in to let you know the electricity is out in your fourplex and it's not because the electric bill wasn't paid.

If you're handling the managing and maintenance of your properties, your first impulse may be to hide because problems are just not fun. But if you've got your network of contractors – a roofer and an electrician and a backup for each in the event the first one you call can't make it– you can pick up the phone and get them out to the locations that need servicing.

If you've been budgeting the maintenance for each of these properties the monthly 4-8% for expenses such as these as suggested in Chapter 6, then you should have no problem covering the costs of these unexpected events.

If the roof is not too old, say between 6-7 years old, it may be time to have it inspected and repair areas that are in need.

Your other property may have an electrical panel that needs replacing, and you haven't really had an inspection done on the property in quite a few years.

This may turn out to be a more expensive proposition, but you need to take action to resolve the issue.

These are unexpected rental expenses that you should have budgeted in the separate accounts for each of the properties.

But what about if your property has a fire? What do you do when the unimaginable happens? What are the things that you need to do in order to mitigate the damage and take care of your tenants, and your property?

Fire and Vacancies

Fire is probably the most disastrous event that can happen to your property. Your tenants are now minus a home to live in and you are now faced with the prospect of months to restore the property if it is salvageable.

<u>Responsibilities After a Fire</u> – This topic is extremely important for you as a landlord. Many landlords do not foresee this type of tragedy happening, but it is real and can happen to any rental owner. For landlords, it is crucial to take the right steps after the fire (Worral, 2018)

This is probably unimaginable to a rental property – fire destroying part or the entire house or building.

Repercussions after the fire are overwhelming and shattering, yet as a landlord, you need to prepare for any type of destruction that may come to the property and your tenants.

The problems you will face after a fire at your rental property can be eased by being educated and well informed on what to do while you begin to try getting the property reestablished and back on the market.

These are steps that should be taken by a landlord directly after a fire, and subsequent weeks after a fire.

Directly After a Fire

- Request a name and contact number from a fire officer for communicating with them for details the insurance company will request

- Immediately file an insurance claim reporting the fire and contacting your insurance agent.

- If you don't already have one, obtain a list from your insurance contact of fire damage restoration companies who are licensed and recommended by them. Within two days, call them and set up an appointment.

- Speak with your tenant asking how they are and check to see that they are safe. Write down anything the tenant may be able to relay about the fire, how it began and anything they took note of just before the fire broke out.

- Have your tenants contact their insurance company to help with temporary housing. Although renters are always encouraged to purchase renter's insurance, there are some tenants who don't. If this is the case, temporary housing and other emergency needs can be taken care of by Constance the American Red Cross.

- Check with the fire officer as to when it will be safe for you and your tenant can get back into the property escorted by fire officials to assess the damage for your information and allowing a tenant to gather necessities and personal property.
  You must have clearance via the fire department that it is safe to enter.

Subsequent Days Post-Fire

- Photos of the damage need to be taken. Include all structures involved

- Make a list and create a list of the damaged or destroyed property. This list should include all the structural damage of the house or building and any other structures on the property like a shed. (Worral, 2018)

- Add details of any structural damage to each room, like cabinets and countertops.

- A separate list should be created for damaged appliances such as a refrigerator or washer and dryer. List the models and types.

- Gather any photos or videos and anything related to the property's structure before the fire. This will give the insurance company an idea of the property and how it looked before the fire, and the destruction after the fire.

- Ask that a report from the fire department provided to you detailing the probable cause of the fire.

- Hold off on removing any debris or begin to repair any of the damage prior to having the fire damage restoration company walk through and take their own photos and inventory of all the damage.

- Lock all doors and windows or cover any open areas with plastic sheeting to secure the property as well as possible.

<u>Questions After a Fire</u> - After a fire, all parties involved enter an unexplored zone as to who has the responsibility to pay for any repairs, and any bills of restoring the property from the fire damage.
Some common questions that are asked:

- Does the tenant have to pay for all the repairs if they were at fault for the fire start?
- Property's insurance deductible – who is responsible to pay for it?

- If the fire was due to landlord neglect, what happens?
- Does the landlord pay for the cost of the tenant's lost belongings?
- Can a landlord fix the fire damage himself?
- If a tenant has to move out temporarily, does the landlord pay for them living somewhere else?
- The rental lease agreement - what happens now?

How a tenant and landlord handle this shocking and upsetting event will depend on how the questions are answered.

This is a time where communication is extremely important, and a certain amount of concern and consideration should be exhibited on both sides so the situation can be handled as smoothly as possible.

Fire Damages – Who Pays? – The ultimate responsibility for the cost of repairing fire damage to the structure, home systems such as plumbing and electrical falls on the landlord.

However, the restoration and repairs don't always have the landlord personally financially responsible. The homeowner's policy the landlord is mandated to carry on the property has no responsibility for replacing, repairing, or paying the lost property of the tenant. (Worral, 2018)

In place to take care of the tenant's loss is a renter's insurance policy covering their belongings such as clothing, furniture, and other property.

If the tenant did not carry renter's insurance, they will experience the result of the loss of their property.

This is why a clause should be included in the lease to protect the tenant's property in such a dire event.

If there is negligence on the part of the landlord that caused the fire to happen and a tenant can prove in court that because of the negligence they lost property, they may have the ability to regain the cost of their lost belongings and any additional expenses in having to arrange to live elsewhere.

If the tenant or a guest of the tenant is at fault for the fire, they will bear the responsibility for the repair of the damage. Although the fire was the fault of the tenant, it is required of the landlord to make preparations for the tenant to reside elsewhere through his homeowner's policy.

If the tenant's policy has liability and the tenant had a partial or total fault of the fire, the landlord's insurance company will seek reimbursement.

Another situation is the landlord's insurance company will look for reimbursement directly from the tenant if they are at fault and have no renter's insurance.

<u>Restoration of Your Property</u> – A landlord has to offer a rental property that is in a condition that is habitable.   The experts that handle the restoration of your property from a fire will provide documentation to you when the property is in the condition to be occupied once again.

In order to protect your investment, get the process for the house fire restoration started as quickly as possible.

Water, smoke, and fire damage can weaken a structure and it doesn't take long for that to occur. Mold and mildew can begin to grow as well within a day after a fire. Immediate action is needed.

Leave the restoration process to the experts!
Never try to restore your property if it's fire-damaged!

A fire damaged structure needs a specific level of proficiency and equipment to make sure that all elements of the structure are restored back into a safe state and is able to meet safety codes at their minimum.

Allowing the experts to handle the restoration also ensures that there are no issues that remain hidden and may arise after the restoration is complete. Having a crew of professional fire restorationists handle the restoring of your rental property is the wise way to go.

To summarize all that has been noted about what happens if a fire damages or destroys your rental property, it would be a good idea to review all the steps a landlord needs to take in the aftershock of a fire well before anything actually occurs. (Worral, 2018)

Vacancies – As with every rental property, a tenant leaving creates a vacancy and there is a period of time you need to have a contingency plan to get new tenants into your rental. (Thorsby, Devon, 2018)

When you're a landlord, there will be a time when your property is vacant and that consistent income becomes inconsistent, the questions is What do you do about it?

Whether your vacancy is because the term of the tenant's lease is up and they moved because they purchased a home of their own, or because you needed to evict the last tenant for non-payment of rent, you need to be able to handle a vacancy financially without putting too much of a dent in your budget for that rental.

Vacancies for rental in the U.S. have been below 10% since 2010. The low vacancy rates are due to a nationwide housing shortage. However, these low vacancy rates are not an assurance that you'll find a tenant after your tenant give notice that they'll be moving.
How long can you sustain a property without tenants?
That's the first thing to know. Then it's leveraging the tenantless period to diminish the likelihood of recurring or lengthy vacancies in the future.

<u>Can you handle a Vacancy?</u> – Vacancy rates are the amount of time over the year you could anticipate your property to be vacant and not collecting rent. If the vacancy rate is 5%, as an example, the property will be vacant a little over 18 days of the year. Basically, you're losing a month's worth of rent over the year if your property is vacant. If the vacancy rate is 14 percent, the property would not be earning an income from the rent for approximately two months, about 51 days.
In order to carry that you need to have a financial cushion to cover the cost of utilities, any necessary repairs, possible renovations and marketing the property for rent for two months. All this without income from a tenant. If you spread this over a year's time with various short-term tenants,

the property could be at three months of rent that's lost. As long as you've budgeted for the vacant months, you can deal with the higher risk. If not, this investment may not be a good one for you to take on. Or, perhaps you are asking too high a rent and need to lower it to help the ability to be rented by more renters who can afford the lower rate.

Seek tenants who have long-term needs – If you don't want to deal with numerous tenants moving in and out of the same rental within a year, note in your rental ad and marketing pieces that you are looking for tenants who want to sign a long-term lease no less than one year. This will ease the stress knowing that there won't be a vacancy for another year, except for any problems that may arise with rent payment or other reasons.

Lower the rent – If your cushion is exhausted and time is running out for your finances, lowering the rent may offer the best decision to get a tenant in place and paying rent.

You may not be generating as much of an income and profit as you had hoped, but even if you're breaking even on the property's expenses, it may be what you need to reconcile for right now. (Thorsby, Devon, 2018)

Dealing with unexpected rental expenses can take a hit on your finances. However, planning ahead and budgeting monthly for episodes that are bound to happen will help ease the financial stress of these types of events.

Hire a Property Manager – This will be covered more fully in Chapter 10.

CHAPTER 10

How to Create a Passive Real Estate Business

Passive Real Estate Business Defined

For some investors that are now in the midst of growing their real estate portfolio, there may be questions they may still have about investing in real estate. They've run the gauntlet of doing all the research and homework necessary to invest in real estate and have purchased their first rental property. Once purchased and made ready to rent, they had it rented. The property is still occupied. The same for the second rental property and possibly a third.

However, investors should know the right questions they should ask if they want to continue building their portfolio that generates a continuous stream of income.
Investing in real estate isn't for everyone who wants to invest. There are questions that you should ask yourself if you wish to take a passive role in real estate investing or a more active one? Will your investing personality type be a fit with rental properties?

Real estate investing that generates a passive income is a strategy that can generate revenue and not actually being energetically participating.

However, the idea of attaining an income isn't as passive as one would think. The level of activity and immersion that is required can vary depending on the type of investment.

This is a misunderstanding that passive income does not require little to no work.

Those who have an interest, as many of you already do, in generating passive revenue investing in real estate need to devise a strategy and have a functional part in a business and should be treated as such.

There is a level of involvement in owning a passive income property whether it's looking through properties, hiring a property manager, having repairs done or screening tenants, especially if an investor wants to increase their profits.

A major component of creating an effective passive investment in real estate comprises developing a solid approach to the business. Accomplishing this comprises an education of the market either in your own neighborhood or other locations.

The data gathered highlights the best market to buy a passive income property and analyze other property listings that have the possibility of good cash flow. (Fortune Builders, 2019)

The research is followed by the execution stage and another plan is needed that will address how your tenants will be managed, the finances of the property and all the paperwork, as well as maintaining and managing the rental property itself.

So, the idea of passive income real estate is more complex than some investors realize and the word passive is NOT the operative word. Unfortunately, some investors only learn the aftermath of purchasing the property and aren't really prepared for the constant day-to-day attention that is needed to just one property, never mind multiples of them.

A sound strategy that can make your real estate investing business work for you and make your life easier will take planning, research, and knowing which questions are the right ones for you to ask and the mistakes you need to avoid.

Passive income real estate is still a good way to attain an additional source of income, develop strategies to achieve financial freedom and reach financial security in your retirement years. Rental properties can develop a consistent revenue stream while having the choice of building equity by making improvements to the property.

However, before you begin, make sure you aren't falling into any of the mistakes that could torpedo the business you have started, or are in the midst of growing:

Mistakes to Avoid

Not enough cash flow – Passive real estate investors will tell you that cash is king. Your main goal when you own rental property is to increase appreciation while simultaneously earning continuous cash flow.

Keep in mind that the real estate market fluctuates and can impact on your appreciation. Your cash flow is the bottom line that provides an income and gives you the ability to maintain your property.

Not prepared to be a landlord – Some newer financially ready investors may decide on that investing in rental properties method attaining revenue while not comprehending it is a difficult and demanding business that can't be handled or taken lightly. You must realize that managing rental property needs to be handled as a small business. (Fortune Builders, 2019)

Not thoroughly screening tenants – In order to make the most of earing a continuous stream of income from investing in real estate is to rent to tenants who are the best qualified.
Bad renters become much more of a financial loss than if the property were vacant. Property damage, or the lengthy process of eviction, or even a lawsuit that is even lengthier can put a drain on your capital.

Not collecting the rent on time - As a landlord, you must be clear to your tenants, and in the lease, they have signed that tenants about rules and that tenant will be held accountable for following them from the beginning.
Some tenants like to think they are able to exploit a landlord who displays being nice, while developing a habit of late payments of the rent or can't make up the rent that is in arrears.
If you wait in collecting rent, the cash flow for the property will suffer as well as create adversity for both the landlord and the tenant which can lead to eviction if the situation is not nipped in the bud.

<u>Not actively participating as a manager</u> – While there may be a property manager maintain your property, you, as an owner, need to actively participate and keep in contact with tenants and making sure there is continued care and upkeep of the rental.

Hiring a property manager seems like a lot of extra time, cost, and effort, but, in the end, it will aid in protecting your finances. When you manage your property in a diligent manner, it can reduce the turnover of tenants, improve the value of the property, and avert avoidable repair costs.

<u>However, how involved in the day to day are you?</u>

Now that we've established that some investors have a misguided idea that creating a passive rental property business takes little to zero work, there are other investors who have learned that the reality is quite the contrary. You, as an investor in rental properties, know that there is a tremendous amount of work that you need for put in order to have a successful and profitable rental property investment enterprise.

One approach you may have your business be a little more passive is to hire a property manager.

Just like hiring a CPA for your bookkeeping and taxes, hiring a property manager is another great investment and one that will save you time and money.

You want to be strategizing your next move in your investments. Should you sell two single-family units and purchase one fourplex? Will a vacancy be better mitigated by spreading a vacancy loss over all units in fourplex?

Hire a Professional Property Manager – It's tempting if you want to save money and try to manage and maintain your properties yourself, or have a family member who doesn't really have property management experience manage your properties. Not a good idea.

In order to have the time to grow your business and not worry that your existing properties are not being managed properly, hiring a professional property manager will free up your time, manage your properties, conduct repairs and maintenance, screen potential tenants and more. (Fortune Builders, 2019)

Property managers are able to seek out tenants when one of your properties develops a vacancy. They will screen the prospective tenants, conduct background checks, take care of all tenant applications, and answer all the questions that a new tenant will have. Over the term of their lease, the property management company will get to know your tenant and will let you know if they are great, or if they're a problem.

They are dedicated to filling your vacant property with new tenants. They are likely to have contact with more marketing outlets, renter networks, and platforms that you would have trying to seek out tenants on a Craigslist ad.

Property managers and their management companies have a network of contractors and handymen at their disposal, many of whom work solely with the management company because it's pretty much-guaranteed work.

Something is always in need of repair at the properties that property management companies maintain and manage.

These contractors are known for their good workmanship because if they don't, the management company will part ways with them.

Your properties and many other investors, owners, and landlords are their clients. Property managers don't want to have shoddy work be your complaint about them.

Another service property managers provide is handling the not-too-pleasant and time-consuming evictions.

Hopefully, the property manager will have done their job and carefully screened all your tenants for your properties.

However, it may be a tenant got laid off from a job, or one of the tenants on the lease leaves and breaches the contract leaving the other tenant holding down the apartment rent that was meant for two people to pay, not just one tenant to pay.

Whatever the case may be, the property manager is professionally trained to handle the eviction, navigating through the courts to get the proper documents filed and having the notice served to the tenants.

Some evictions are more difficult than others and, because they are aware of the temperament of some of the tenants, may have to have assistance having them removed from the premises.

An eviction can take up to 45-60 days.

Be aware that court calendars for this type of court proceeding are usually full, and if there is a holiday that closes the court, you may have to wait a longer period of time.

Of course, this doesn't help your ability to re-rent the property. However, property managers are well aware of what a vacancy means to your finances and do everything possible to help you during this stressful process.

Although it behooves every investor to be aware of the laws of the State, cities, and municipalities where their properties are located, property managers are dedicated on a daily basis to keep up with any changes in the law and the trends that can affect your rental property investments.

(Fortune Builders, 2019)

Realize that a management company charges to maintain rental properties. Usually, they charge 10% of the monthly rental income to manage the property.

For example, if you are renting a property at $1,500 per month, the property management company will be paid $150 per month. This is how much it will cost to make your property a passive income investment.

Check with the property management company about how much they will charge monthly because this will affect your monthly bottom line.

Ways to Create Passive Income

<u>Single-family</u> - As a real estate property investor, you have made investments in rental properties that can be single-family homes, condominiums, and townhomes.

The benefits and disadvantages of these types of rental properties have been covered throughout this book.

<u>Duplexes, triplexes and more</u> - Some investors have moved on to duplexes, triplexes and more. These are beneficial because a vacancy deficit can be spread out over three or four units versus only one.

This type of real estate can be a bit harder to oversee than a sole residence because of the increased number of tenants. However, they provide better cash flow potential.

<u>Apartment buildings</u> – This is a building classification that applies to rental properties with five or more units. Instead of a residential loan, an investor can apply for a commercial loan.

An apartment building demands more demanding management or hires a professional property manager.

<u>Commercial buildings</u> – Retail tenants can obtain long-term leases in commercial buildings which promises more continuous cash flow.

Be advised that tenants of commercial properties highly customize the property to their needs and can be more difficult to replace in the event they go out of business.

If you invest in commercial buildings, have a plan that projects for longer vacancies in addition to absorbing the expenditure remodeling space.

<u>Industrial complexes</u> – Residential properties usually come to mind when passive income is mentioned. However, don't ignore properties that are modified to the commercial segment.

Warehouses, manufacturing facilities and other types of industrial facilities are all commercial properties that can generate steady performance and not require as much managing. Keep in mind the turnover of tenants usually generates longer vacancies.

Mixed-use developments – Mixed-use developments are in demand and have increased progressively. These developments can offer rental space for a variety of different types of businesses - retail, and industrial, office and residential can be considered for this type of development.

A diverse stream of revenue and long leases can pique an investor's interest and appreciation.

Mobile home parks – This type of rental is an appealing option of housing that can be offered to residents who are stressed economically or where housing prices have risen steeply.

Investors own the land of a mobile home park. Tenants pay for the convenience of having a mobile home in the park. Investing in mobile home parks is lucrative. Multiple partnerships or part of a fund is how investors frequently go into the deal.

Self-storage facilities – Investing in a self-storage facility is in high demandable to be located practically in any part of the U.S. The costs span a number of units. This makes each unit low in cost, as well as balancing the cost of any vacancy.

There is a need to have a team managing this type of facility frequently having staff on hand for extended hours.

Additional expenses to factor are insurance and security expenses.

Land Lots – Land can be a little complex, as it doesn't generate income while it sits empty. This type of investment can be a niche investment and used to improve or sold as smaller lots when it's split up.

If the land is in a growing area or is soon to be developed, it can be an effective investment and will sell at a profit.

You can also own timberland or farmland that you can rent out.

Vacation rentals – This type of property may be good for short-term or vacation rentals. Vacation rentals can have higher rental charges than they would with a tenant renting for the long-term. The rental rate is based per-night.

The downside of vacation rentals is the continuous scheduling, cancellations, housekeeping services, and a higher vacancy rate during the off-season.

REITs (Real Estate Investment Trusts) – As a mutual fund, REITs These offers an individual the opportunity to invest in real estate and remain totally inactive in the day-to-day of a rental property.

High-end or commercial properties are the target of REITs

Tax Liens – When taxes on a property are not paid, the government takes hold of the property giving investors the opportunity to purchase properties that have tax liens. They can be purchased at a substantial discount.

The buying and selling of these notes have a large market surrounding these notes, some of which have not been paid over a period of time. Performing notes can be purchased by investors.

Other Ways to Make Passive Income

If you want to invest in real estate and make a passive income, there are some other ways to do so. Owning a brick and mortar property is what many investors envision when they think of real estate that will earn them a passive income, but there are other ways to do this.

You don't have to own an individual piece of property in order and as has been previously stated in the chapter, not everyone is cut out to be a landlord.

Even with a property management company taking the reins, some investors felt there is too much involved and shy away from that end of the business. Some investors would rather purchase real estate properties, renovate, and repair them and then flip them making short-term profits rather than deal with tenants and issues that can arise with rental properties.

CROWDFUNDING

The investment world has evolved regarding investing in real estate. You don't have to own limited to owning commercial or residential rentals directly.

To earn a passive income investing in real estate, you have other choices. Investing in real estate via Crowdfunding is an option.

Crowdfunded companies are comparable to peer-to-peer lending, offering a program will match investors with a selection of investments like Prosper and Lending Club.

They assist people who are seeking to invest in real estate passively. Additionally, investors don't have to bargain with sellers. The tractor of ownership of the properties is managed, allowing the investor the freedom of little to no involvement in the properties.

These programs are a good way to make an investment and derive a passive income from real estate. You can accomplish this and not have to invest or take out a loan for vast amounts of money or be the sole owner of the investment.

All the work that takes so much time and is the responsibility of the sole owner of a property who responsible for it is something that you can forego when crowdfunding.

There are two groups of people that crowdfunding is made available - accredited investors and non-accredited investors. Further in this chapter, these two groups will be explained. (Blank, 2019)

There are various crowdfunded companies. Each operates differently and has specific standards that investors need to adhere to.

<u>Rich Uncles</u> – Buy shares of a REIT (Real Estate Investment Trust) in housing for students for as low as $5.00.

Almost anyone can get started investing with this low investment amount. https://www.richuncles.com/

Rich Uncles uses crowdfunding and makes investing in real estate available to everyone.

In their REIT choices, the properties are commercial real estate properties and student housing properties.

The choice is totally up to the investor whether they wish to invest in one or both of the two REIT offerings.

BRIX REIT - Centers on student housing. Properties are purchased to house college students that are located the walking distance of a mile from major universities.

Minimum to invest is $5.00

NNN REIT – This works a little differently with Rich Uncles. It requires $500, which is the minimum that can be invested. Industrial properties, office buildings, and retail are what this REIT zeroes in on.

REIT I – Available to investors already existing with Rich Uncles. Office buildings, retail, and industrial properties.

Nationally recognized tenants lease to both NNN REIT and the REIT I lease.

The goal is to lease these properties to tenants who have solid financial statements and income history. A Bonus – Rich Uncles charges no fees, cutting the middleman out so the investor can save money.

Investor Criteria – There are no accredited investor criteria Rich Uncles, although it is asked that an investor has a minimum of a family income of $75,000 or a net worth of $250,000.

Rich Uncles saves investors' money by not charging broker fees, monthly dividends paid with the ability to cash them out or have them reinvested.

The choice is investors.

If you're a beginner in real estate investing, the low minimum investment and no fees are attractive to start with.

Fundrise – Fundrise is an online platform of real estate investing. Founded in 2010. This crowdfunding company has an investment minimum of $500 and focuses on commercial property in what they call eREITs. eREIT is a mix of REITs that are traded on the exchange and non-traded REITs.
https://fundrise.com/

The savings are Fundrise and the eREITs. Fundrise's eREIT charges low fees which is one of the main benefits to an investor. (Blank, 2019)

Conventional REITs have high fees, sometimes 15% or higher. This is not the case with Fundrise eREIT which comes with 1% of the annual management fee.

Like other REITs that are not traded, Fundrise's eREIT doesn't waver when the stock market does. It is less susceptible to the swings that the stock market goes through.

Investor criteria – Investors wanting to invest with Fundrise can review the eREIT investment funds and determine which they find most suitable for them.

Fundrise wants to do away with the middleman, such as brokers who charge fees to investors. Fundrise ensures their REIT profits go to investors directly.

There is one major way that Fundrise differs from other crowdfunding companies.

The minimum investment is $500. This is a cost that makes it affordable for almost anyone who wants to invest in real estate and earn a passive income.

Investors won't be going through a broker when buying a Fundrise eREIT product, but instead will be buying directly, the reason Fundrise charges a low fee.

Each offering is defined on its website. Additionally, investors are alerted when there is an addition of new assets to the eREITs that they have an investment.

There are four different eREITs that are currently available to investors who are new:

- Starter Portfolio
- Supplemental Income Portfolio
- Balanced Investing Portfolio
- Long-term Growth Portfolio

An investor can invest in any of the eREITs Fundrise provides.

Realty Mogul – An investor is investing in real estate by purchasing one of their LLCs shares of stock. The LLC then invests in another LLC where the property title is held. https://www.realtymogul.com/

Realty Mogul minimizes the overhead by running the business in this manner. Additionally, investors have access to more investment selections. (Blank, 2019)

Minimum investment requirement is $1,000.

An investor is usually buying stock shares with Realty Mogul. There is an extensive variety of properties for investment that they can buy:

- Office buildings
- Medical buildings
- Self-storage facilities
- Multi-family dwellings
- Industrial sites
- Single-family investments

Realty Mogul offers equity and loan investments.

Loan investment terms are 6-12 months. Longer-term equity investments run 3-10 years. The investments are accessible to accredited investors.

REITs are also offered to non-accredited investors. Multi-family dwellings are one of the focuses of Realty Mogul. Others offer a diversity of commercial real estate.

Investor Criteria – Realty Mogul permits both accredited and non-accredited investors to invest. Non-accredited investors can only invest in MogulREIT 1 and MogulREIT 2.

Realty Mogul account fees are 0.50% and 0.60% annually. Profits are dispersed quarterly or monthly.

The company has a vetting process that is complicated and approves only 10% of deals they are offered and won't lend money haphazardly which is good for their investors.

stREITwise – Commercial real estate is managed by this crowdfunded-type REIT. An investor gets access to a portfolio of private real estate assets that are professionally managed. https://streitwise.com/

$1,000 is the minimum investment with stREITwise, a very affordable level.

When an investor makes their initial investment in stREITwise, it is held for at least one year. When the year is up, the investor is able to cash in shares on a quarterly basis.

Mixed-use and office buildings are the primary investments. stREITwise REIT has shown annual returns averaging ten percent to date.

Investor Criteria – Investors who are both accredited and non-accredited are open to investing, although non-accredited investors are subjected to investment stipulations to stREITwise.

Non-credited investors must invest less than 10% of their total net worth. The net worth cannot include their home. Additionally, they also have to invest less than ten percent of their annual income. (Blank, 2019)

These rules are set for the protection of non-accredited investors from over-investing.

Upfront fees are 3% and a continual 2% annual management fee is withdrawn before there is dividend distribution.

These fees may be high, but in reality, they're not.

Actually, they're lower than what many REITs charges.

stREITwise is honest and open about these fees and that's the difference.

No hidden fees at stREITwise.

What is an Accredited Investor – An accredited investor is one who meets a particular financial benchmark. Crowdfunded companies are rigid concerning who they permit to invest through their company and do this to safeguard other investors. Accredited investors are to meet the criteria of:

- Having have $200,000 income or have a $300,000 joint income with a spouse. The minimum income needs to have been met over the past two years and expected to be continuing in the present year.

- Must have $1 million or more like net worth, and not include their primary residence. The net worth can be a joint account with their spouse or sole investments and savings.

If an investor meets either of these criteria, they are an accredited investor. If not, then you are considered a non-accredited investor.

Non-accredited investors are not as wealthy and cannot meet the criteria and the effect suffering a loss of an investment would be impactful. This is the reason why only accredited investors are allowed to invest in some of the crowdfunding companies.

REITS

A REIT (real estate investment trust) is a passive real estate investment income, comparable to a mutual fund. REITs have a varied number of diverse investments housed in each fund.

Real estate is what makes the distinction of these REITs investments.

For example, a REIT may contain a number of diverse investment types that are owned:

- Shopping malls
- Timberland
- Warehouses
- Commercial office buildings

These are just a few that are named. There are many diverse types of real estate properties the REIT can contain.

There is more risk of investing in one real estate property, much like investing in a single-family rental home.

There is less risk for an investor with a variety of investments in REITs. The investor isn't putting their eggs in one basket.

REITs can be private, exchange-traded, and non-traded. An exchange-traded REIT can be purchased with any broker who is registered with the SEC (Securities Exchange Commission) with regular reports filed with the SEC.

Exchange-traded REITs are listed on national securities exchanges like the NYSE or Nasdaq.

There is a disadvantage to trading a REIT on the exchange. Primarily, an REIT's performance can be similar to the performance of the exchange it's listed on.

As an example, if a REIT that is listed on the NYSE (New York Stock Exchange) and the exchange drops, the value of the REIT could drop as well.

REITs that are Non-Traded – REITs that are non-traded operate somewhat differently. As it's been stated, an exchange-traded REIT is listed on the SEC. Its files company trading reports with the SEC as does exchange-traded REITs.

The difference is the non-traded REITs do not get traded on an exchange and they are not publicly traded.

An illiquid asset is what a non-traded REIT is called, meaning that it is harder to sell off than a non-traded REIT.

However, both kinds of REITs are forms of passive real estate investing.

Private REITs – A private REIT are investments that are not listed on the SEC. They may have more risk than the other options because they have no connection with the SEC.

There are varied options for investing in real estate. Learn the details of the diverse real estate investment options that are available. Consider those options to determine which one would be the best one for you. If you do, real estate is a feasible investment selection.

Other crowdfunding companies - Visit the websites of these other crowdfunding companies (Blank, 2019)

EQUITYMULTIPLE - https://www.equitymultiple.com/
Roofstock – https://www.roofstock.com/
CrowdStreet - https://www.crowdstreet.com/

CONCLUSION

You've made it through Rental Property Investing –
The Essentials for Experienced Investors - How to Build a Smart
and Unshakeable Wealth to the end.
Congratulations!
Hopefully, it was informative and able to provide you with all of
the tools you need to achieve the goals you are striving for.

Many people have good intentions of reading the book but don't
get through the book to its end. The title may be intriguing, and
they buy the book, read one or two chapters, and then they
become distracted, never to pick up the book again.

You may be well into growing your real estate investment
business and now have quite a few properties that are rentals.
By having read this book, it appears you are a serious real estate
investor continuing to grow your business and learning more
about becoming a good landlord for your tenants.
The information contained in this book is very valuable and may
answer some of the questions that have come up for you in the
process of running both your businesses.

On the investment end, the cost of doing business changes from
being a market that is a hot buyer's market or when a seller's
market slows you down and you need to know the best ways to
gauge your capital and understand how your profits may be
affected. Real estate is a volatile business.
Hopefully, both your businesses will continue to thrive, generate
the profits you wish to gain, and you will have a smoothly
running real estate business in investing and ownership.

And please leave me a honest/sincere comment about the content, I will certainly read it and will help me to enrich my knowledge about my audience, and for sure it will be useful for other readers like you.
I thank you in advance.

Lightning Source UK Ltd.
Milton Keynes UK
UKHW021850161220
375343UK00008B/487